# Navigating Through Clown World
## (A Laypersons Perspective...)

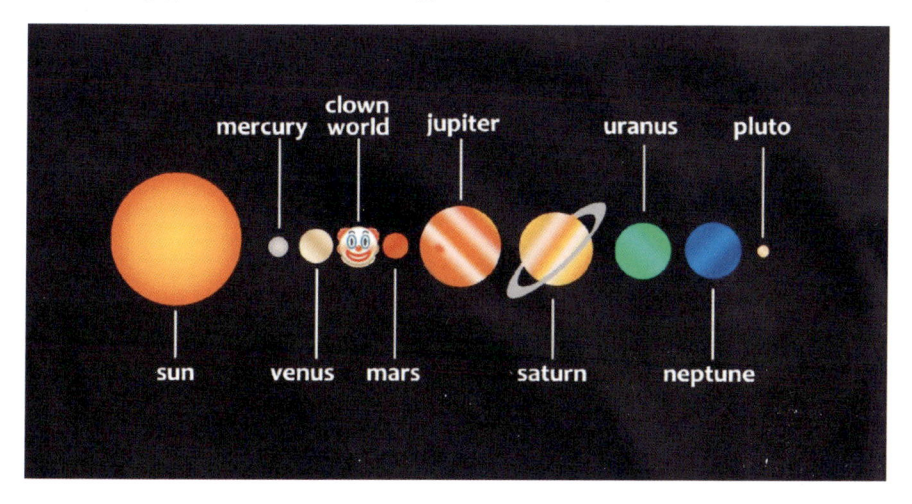

Written By Dan Lewis BSc Hons Fitness, health & Nutrition / Top Postie

# Prelude

We all remember the days pre-March 2020 when we were all getting on with our lives quite happily with our mundane yet relatively prosperous existence. Blissfully unaware of most political rhetoric or propaganda. Naively thinking ideologies such as communism, totalitarianism and fascism were all banished to the depths of the history books, unthinkable that they'd ever make a return. What most of us didn't realise was that tyranny throughout time is actually the norm, not the exception; our current western democracy is just a relative fart in the wind in terms of human existence. Before the early 1900's society was literally all tyranny, we've been very lucky to have been alive during this point in history! We all assumed democracy was never going to end, it was here to stay, most of us never dreamt that our democracy would end in our lifetime or thought there was a possibility that our democracy is merely an illusion and we just weren't aware. This book is link referenced and also interactive with video links, bear in mind that documents and studies are becoming increasingly censored. If the links fail to work in the future, go to https://archive.org and try the links there. All opinions are my own, derived from my independent research and observable reality, I don't expect you to agree with everything and I've obviously missed or overlooked certain issues, my main aim is to get you thinking outside of the box at other potential narratives.

I would like to this opportunity to thank my daughter Myah for keeping me relatively sane during my journey through clown world, at 11 years old she is wise beyond her years and verifiably a rock to my continued wellness and mental health, thanks Mooey! She's also the reason I'm so passionate about the subject matter and to ensure her and her generation have a prosperous and free future that everyone deserves.

First off, I'll go over some terms that you may not be familiar with that will spring up from time to time for the duration of this book….

"**Clown World**" – Planet Earth as we've known it since March 2020 to the present day (early 2023)

"**Normie**" – The average low IQ person who unquestionably buys into all mainstream political rhetoric and propaganda of the day.

"**Based**" – An individual awake to alternative narratives, someone who sees through propaganda and who is unaffected by social engineering.

"**The Matrix**" – Our slave scam system of Debt, Tax, Laws & Authority, which the 1999 film of the same name metaphorically nails.

# Contents

**Chapter 1 - Clown World Begging's...** Page 4

**Chapter 2 - Vaccines our Saviour?**... Page 8

**Chapter 3 - Casedemic, Masks & Cults**... Page 18

**Chapter 4 - Clown World Policy & Politically Correct 'Wokeness'**... Page 26

**Chapter 5 - Scams & More Scams**... Page 38

**Chapter 6 - What's Happening? Why? & What Can We Do?**... Page 52

## Chapter 1 - Clown World Beginnings

March 2020 started like any other March, my daughter had her birthday on the 4th and had a party with her friends. Work was pretty normal, the usual jokes and banter with my colleges. As usual I had a good relationship with my family and friends, things were just normal, as they always had been. Then out of nowhere the media and news is full of stories of a deadly disease coming out of Wuhan China, people falling down dead in the streets, people in full hazmat suits cleaning the mess (V1), I'm not going to lie, it looked bad. But I'm not the worrying type and knew these things usually get hyped way out of proportion by the media, so I assumed it would blow over fairly quickly just like it had with every other crisis in my lifetime such as the mad cow disease, swine flu, bird flu, Zica, anthrax, hell, even the millennium bug! I laughed it off with my workmates telling them to chill out, that was until videos of huge temporary hospitals being erected started circulating on social media, apparently to cater to the huge amount of incoming sick patients. These videos were circulating for days, my colleges were constantly posting similar content to our private chat groups and messages, even my dad sent me a video of a guy supposedly ill with covid saying that the disease was horrendous and felt like razor blades in your lungs, My Brother was telling me 1 in 4 people who contract covid were dying, it was at this point I thought, OK something bad might be happening here....

Fast-forward a couple of days and our Prime minister Boris Johnson had announced that we, as a nation were copying the Communist China model and we would lockdown for 15 days to flatten the curve of the virus. Being a normie at the time, I believed it to be an acceptable precaution and had no reason to question it. That day my daughter had been sent home from school for having a high temperature, a pretty general procedure. The next day at work I mentioned to a couple of my colleges that my daughter had been sent home with a temperature the previous day, to my amazement one of my colleges literally started frothing from the mouth in rage and demanded that I leave the premises immediately and if I didn't, he'd stage a walk out from the office. Little did I know this was actually the official guidelines from the government, my manager sent me home to the delight of my cowardice work college and I had 10 days paid leave. I don't know if you remember but April of 2020 was clear skies, 20ish degree heat and summer like weather. 10 days in the garden with my daughter it was, for the first time in a while I had time to burn, this led me to start looking into lockdowns, Covid-19 and questioning the official narrative, I guess you could say it was actually the start of my own personal awakening, little did I know, I was about to start my exit from the matrix.

Being a bachelor of science and having a degree I did have some prior knowledge of reading and dissecting scientific papers, I knew exactly what makes a strong paper and what makes a weak paper. A dead giveaway of a poor scientific paper is if it has a small sample size and also if there are no randomised controls. I always remember the first thing I was taught at university is that you never conclude during scientific research, you only ever hypothesis and promote ideas for further research. Finding something untrue is far more powerful than stating something to be a fact, it takes a lifetime of experiments to prove me correct but only one to prove me wrong. These specific learning's would stay in my mind during my future research, the terms "Trust the Science" & "Follow the Science" remember them? We'll get to that later….

Initially, I started looking into lockdowns, to my horror it became apparent that lockdowns weren't part of any nation's previous influenza pandemic precautions guidelines or protocols (1), they were actually an extreme fringe pseudoscientific militarised approach, usually confined to Hollywood zombie movies and prisons. In fact, they completely contradicted all public health and epidemiological practice and theory. My first thought was that maybe the government panicked, anyway it was only for 15 days, or so I thought. In the back of my mind, I couldn't help but think something nefarious was at play, nothing quite added up. Those 10 days went by quickly and I was back to work, being a key worker, I worked through all lockdown periods (baring my initial 10-day absence). I was working for Royal Mail, our workload reached absolutely insane volumes, I mean it was like Christmas time in our sorting office for the best part of a year. Strangely the public were buying predominantly clothes and shoes not essential items, which seemed strange given they couldn't go out!

I remember all the posties conferring that it's crazy that we have to continue to work while everyone else was locked up for their own safety, why were we not being treated with the same precaution as other professions? It was very confusing times for all of us. Just to note, for those first 7 months at the height of the pandemic, we were working in close contact, indoors and sharing vans outdoors, giving parcels and mail to 100's of people per day, we weren't masking, we were just given hand sanitizer and a bit of distancing while in the office. Not one postie contracted covid for the best part of 18 months, well, that was before the testing began but nobody got sick, not one.

I remember walking the streets in those first few weeks, it was like a scene out of some crap dystopian movie, not a soul to be seen anywhere. You had people who were too terrified to open the door to receive a parcel and then you had others who would pat you on the back and tell you "Well done, keep up the good work". It really was such a strange time, with nobody really knowing how to behave or how to act, one thing was for sure, the media wanted everyone as scared as possible and the majority were petrified. It was at this point I started questioning the media narrative, every day when I got home from work the TV was bombarding me, stating how bad covid was and how many were sick. However, I was out there every day working and apart from the pantomime of people wearing masks and not wanting to answer the door, the pandemic didn't seem observable in the slightest. I worked out of a small town in Devon known to us as 'Gods waiting room' due to the average age of the local population, as far as I'm aware not one of my elderly customers passed on during those months, the whole thing just seemed off to me. Just to note I've noticed plenty have now passed in recent months after the booster roll out.

During the next few weeks, the notorious PCR covid tests became available, my work manager needed someone to drive around East Devon and pick up these PCR tests from the homes of people suspected of having the virus and bring them back to the mail centre where they'd be sent off for examination. At this point due to my own observations and distrust in the official narrative, I wasn't scared in the slightest so put myself forward for the job. For the next 6 weeks I was driving around East Devon collecting PCR tests in my van. At this point still completely mask less, again I found people's reactions to my presence increasingly very odd. Some people would answer the door and pat me on the back before giving me their test, some elderly people were so confused with the process of administering the test that I'd have to wait and show them how to administer the test myself, some people weren't even in and their kids handed me the test at the door, some would make me stand clear while they put the test on the floor, then made me wait until their door was firmly closed before they'd allow me pick up the test, I'm still not sure who they were trying to protect, I thought they were supposed to be the ones with covid, not me, strange logic! The whole scenario was clearly starting to play with people's minds, it was like they couldn't think straight, and common sense was truly a rare occurrence during this period. Up until this period the government had declared that a vaccine may not even be possible, and then as if by magic 4/5 Big Pharma companies all came up with a vaccine at the exact same time. Again, like with lockdowns I hit the books and searched the internet for studies on mRNA vaccines as well as the history of modern vaccination. This was my first taste of censorship and suppressed information, you really had to dig deep to find any notable information, Google and other search engines make it very hard by way of using an algorithm to hide or at least push down in the results the information you're looking for, luckily my autistic traits and with the help of the Wayback machine enabled me to keep digging further. After looking into the development of RNA and mRNA vaccines and their role in other coronaviruses with a higher IFR such as SARS and MERS, it became clear that study after study stemming back from the 1960's, all the way up until the early 2000's had all ended after animal trials. The reason was that within these studies the animals all developed autoimmune enhancement deficiency better known as ADE, at a later date, many of which died. What happened was that the vaccines seemed to be successful initially, that was until the animals were re-infected with the wild strain of the virus? Their immune system didn't recognise the threat and it entered their body like a Trojan horse. To my knowledge they never fixed this problem and the studies came to an abrupt halt around 2002 until they reappeared around 2019. One study concluded that caution should be taken with this kind of vaccine development within humans (2).

At this point I was starting to call bullshit on the whole narrative and decided to make an Instagram post stating my experience and the information I had researched, the overwhelming reaction was positive, like myself, many others were clearly questioning the narrative, although, for the first time my colleges were starting to ridicule me because of my views and my family and friends started referring to me as a 'conspiracy theorist', a term I'd always assumed was reserved for individuals who believed in aliens and bigfoot. Nowadays apparently a 'conspiracy theorist' is a term used for anyone daring to question the official narrative, I thought to myself, "so, I'm a conspiracy theorist just because you won't research?", buy hey, ignorance is bliss, I'll cover this more in depth later…

## Chapter 2 – Vaccines our Saviour?

My manager had recently become aware of my Instagram post and removed me from my PCR test collections, to be honest I think he thought I had gone a crazy, by the way, this guy was the epitome of a slave mind normie, a fat, junk eating lazy slob who went out of his way to bully people for no apparent reason. Anyway, now I'm back in the office, the vaccine appointments are being rolled out to the most vulnerable. Their appointment letters are coming thick and fast and we have to treat them like a special delivery. For those who don't know, a special delivery is the highest-grade postal item, it has to be delivered that day and kept secure at all times.

My mother and farther were due for their jabs, both in their late 60's and early 70's, separated and divorced since I was six and have other children from other relationships. My mother, a free spirited and open minded individual, my father, more academic, a former University tutor. I had decided it wasn't my place to try and sway their decision in regards of vaccination, although I did go over the infection fatality rates with them, it was very low, even for their age group, around 0.1% (3). Knowing this information my mother declined her shots and my father, now retired and sitting in front of the BBC propaganda machine day in day out, decided he needed multiple.

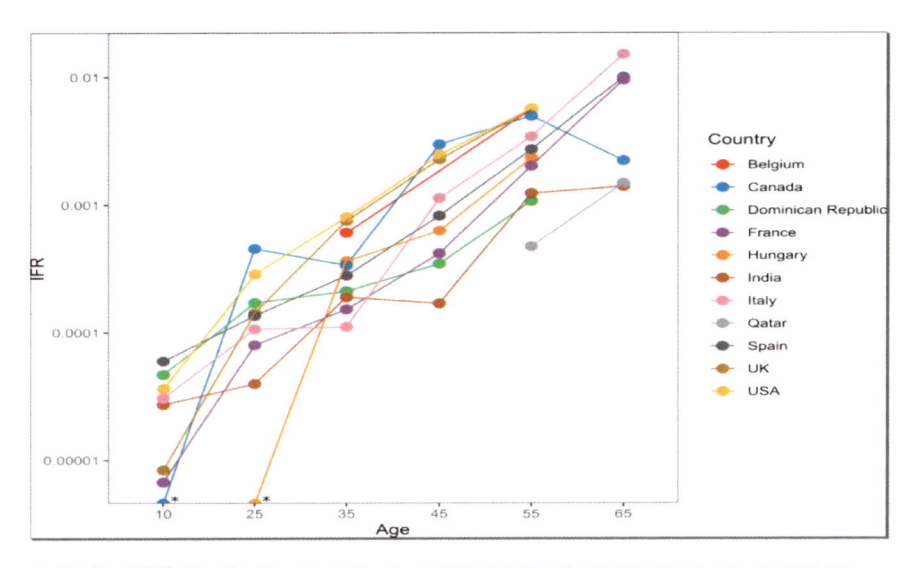

**Figure 3. Infection fatality rates in younger age groups derived from included seroprevalence studies.**
IFRs are corrected for unmeasured antibody types. Sample size weighted IFRs were calculated for countries with multiple estimates available. * Infinite values produced by zero death counts.

As time progressed the vaccine rollout continued, eventually it got to my age group, at the time I was in my late 30's so my infection fatality rate was virtually non-existent, however authorities had ramped up their coercion and were now pushing the notion that the vaccine was not just for your own safety, but it was for others safety too i.e., it would stop you passing the virus onto others and stop transmission in it's tracks. In the UK they rolled out a "Vaccinate to Save Granny" advertising campaign, there were also other advertising campaigns such as "Stay Home, Save Lives" and other catchy slogans that stuck with you. Very strange that they'd need a number of campaigns for a supposedly deadly disease, in fact the UK government spent close to £500m of tax payers money trying to scare the population into vaccine submission. Also how many times did we hear for the greater good on the news and from politicians, straight out of Nazi rhetoric and propaganda.

**IF YOU GO OUT, YOU CAN SPREAD IT. PEOPLE WILL DIE.**

STAY HOME ▸ PROTECT THE NHS ▸ SAVE LIVES

I decided to go down the rabbit hole on the reasons behind this blatant vaccine coercion. Bear in mind I'm a fully childhood vaccinated individual and so is my daughter, this is what I uncovered...

Having previously looked into the mRNA and RNA vaccines I decided to look closer at the history of all vaccines and the people/organisations behind the vaccination rollout. To be honest I'd never had reason to look into any of this kind of thing in the past and what I found was truly perspective changing.

What became apparently clear almost immediately was that any kind of medical coercion was completely illegal under the Nurenberg Code, which was written into law after the atrocities of Nazi scientists at the end of the 2$^{nd}$ World War. The media and government weren't offering any common-sense health advice, I'd go as far to say they were suppressing it. Being a graduate of a health and fitness degree, I was well aware of the correlation between vitamin deficiencies, being overweight or unfit and fatality rates. Why weren't the government promoting a healthy diet, vitamin supplements such as Vitamin-D and Zinc which has always been known to help with disease immunity? All they were offering was the binary option of a vaccine, an experimental one at that, which most of the population didn't even need. As well as ignoring common sense health advice they seemed to completely ignore natural immunity, natural immunity was already being shown to be far more robust than vaccine immunity (4) and a growing number of doctors were calling the government out on their nonsensical policies and health advice or lack thereof. Nearly 1 million public health scientists signed the Great Barrington Declaration (5) voicing their concerns with the damaging physical impacts of Covid policy, they recommend an approach called focused protection which is what all nations pre-covid pandemic protocols and response systems were based on, it was also the approach the nation of Sweden took. Contrary to mainstream narrative, Sweden didn't lockdown at all, they advised that the elderly and vulnerable protected themselves and that everyone else was entitled to judge their own risk factors. Masking, lockdowns, business closure and vaccines were never mandated, they were only optional at your own discretion (6). Initially Sweden had the same surge in cases and deaths as other nations but has since not had the huge non covid excess deaths that other nations experienced due to draconian lockdown measures. We can only guess at the reason for these post covid excess deaths (the media refuse to cover it) but you'd think it was probably mental health issues occurring because of isolation and having your business shut down, leading to suicide. Missed doctors' appointments, people were either too scared to leave their house for an appointment or appointments simply weren't available, health services seemed to negate disease with a much higher fatality rate such as cancer and heart disease, while their sole focus was covid. Lastly, there was vaccine damage and deaths which the media, like with common sense health advice, decided to completely ignore, apparently because it would lead to vaccine hesitancy, you think?! I was checking the VAERS database in the UK and US regularly and could see a huge spike in injury and deaths after vaccination (7) at the time of writing the UK VAERS data has recorded 1.4 million entries which includes 32,000 deaths and 60,000 permanent disabilities by way of covid vaccination, that's just the UK figures. It's worth noting that the swine flu vaccination rollout was ended after 17 deaths. The VAERS database had previously been shown to cover around 1-10% of the actual entries (8). This supposedly due the complexity of filling out the document, as well as doctors being hesitant to claim the vaccine as injury causation, again due to not wanting to promote vaccine hesitancy and then there's funding, pharmaceutical lobbying and system protocols, we'll talk more on that later.

I decided to explore the company's manufacturing the vaccines, let me tell you, these companies have criminal activity and lawsuits stretching back as long as they've been in business. Pfizer seems to be the worst culprit; they had received the largest fine in medical history amongst many others and were ordered by the department of justice to pay $2.3 billion dollars for fraudulent marketing (9). They were caught marketing the drug Bextra as an anti-inflammatory which was doing the exact opposite, causing inflammation and causing sickness and injury, amazingly the FDA had previously cleared this drug as safe and effective, you've heard that line before!

Next, we have Johnson & Johnson who had previously been fined and ordered to pay $2.2 billion dollars. The reason for this fine was off-label marketing and kickbacks to doctors and pharmacists (10). That's right, they were caught giving financial incentives to doctors to promote and prescribe dangerous medication which had not been cleared by the FDA.

Finally, we have AstraZeneca. Now I have a funny story behind this one. My sister had previously told me that AstraZeneca was the best option because they're in partnership with The University of Oxford and that they're all nerds who wouldn't dream of being complicit in corruption, the naivety! Anyway, one look into their previous conduct and yep, you guessed it, a $550 million dollar fine amongst others for illegally promoting drugs which weren't safe of effective, this time the anti-psychotic drug Seroquel (11), are you starting to see a connection here?! A lot more data is now available than it was back then thanks to the freedom of information act. AstraZeneca were ordered to release injury data on their vaccine (12), take a look for yourself, I can tell you it's not for the faint hearted. Instead of holding these companies and people funding these companies accountable, in true clown world fashion the director of the Oxford Vaccine Group, Andrew Pollard, and the chief executive officer of AstraZeneca, Pascal Soriot, were knighted in the Queen's birthday honours list. Effectively indemnifying them from prosecution in UK courts, go figure.

Recently Pfizer were also ordered to release their original vaccine trial data, also due to the freedom of information act. It should be noted that they had tried to bury this data for 75 years, they initially asked to release

500 pages per month which would take 75 years for the total release, nothing to hide then! Unfortunately for them they were ordered to release 12,000 pages initially with 55,000 more released there after each month until the total 300,000 pages were fully disclosed. Can I point you to pages 7 and 12 of the referenced documents (13) For those who want to carry on reading for now, there were 1200 deaths during the trial alone and 238 pregnancies experienced problems out of 270 pregnant subjects, sounds safe to me!

What's worse these companies with a criminal history longer than the river Nile have indemnity and wouldn't face legal action or consequences in regards to vaccine injury, the reason is that these vaccines have an emergency use clearance. Emergency use clearance is only enabled providing no known treatments are available. I've not looked into this to a great extent but from what I have read and watched it seems there is profound evidence that a number of treatments were supressed that front line doctors stated had positive effects on severity of symptoms and prevented deaths. Most notably Ivermectin, Hydroxychloroquine, Monoclonal Antibodies and even high doses of Vitamin D3, Zinc and Quercetin. Doctor Peter Mccullough, one of the most cited cardiologists in history reported very early on that these protocols had significant benefit and could have potentially saved 1000's of lives had they received early preventive treatment before they arrived at hospital, instead of his findings being promoted, true to the current clown world ideology, he was censored, ridiculed and had his medical license removed. I'd advise everyone to watch his podcast interview with Joe Rogan (V2) he reference everything he says with peer reviewed studies yet was called a dangerous spreader of misinformation in the media, personally I don't think it takes a genius to be able to differentiate between a knowledgeable experienced doctor and a tyrannical establishment puppet, see anything by Anthony Fauci for the latter, the guy is the epitome of the clown world with more contradictions than you'd think imaginable. What's worse most slave mind normies buy his propaganda, love it, and then defend it! We'll hear more about this Fauci character in the coming chapters.

Strangely enough, if you look into the funding of these vaccine companies, one certain organisation seems to be the top donor, every time, The Bill & Melinda Gates Foundation (14). Mr Gates did a Ted talk presentation pre covid on the dangers of the next incoming pandemic, what a visionary! How did he know? He went onto state that he could lower the population with more vaccines (V3), probably nothing! We'll cover more on Mr Bill Gates in much more detail as we progress.

**ALJAZEERA** ● LIVE

News | Coronavirus pandemic

### Which countries have stopped using AstraZeneca's COVID vaccine?

*Concerns grow over reports of blood clotting among some recipients, but WHO urges countries to keep using the COVID vaccine.*

**MailOnline | Health**

### Astrazeneca took a MONTH to turn over coronavirus vaccine trial data to the FDA after a participant's rare spinal complication triggered a pause

By Mary Kekatos Senior Health Reporter For Dailymail.com
15:36, 15 Oct 2020 , updated 18:43, 20 Oct 2020

52 shares

26 comments

At this point I had little to no confidence in these vaccine companies. I was interested to see if this kind of tyrannical policy and crony corruption had a place in vaccine history. At first using Google as my search engine all the articles and documents I could find stated vaccines were the saviour of infectious disease and that vaccine science was unequivocal. Obviously, this was my normie perception through the years but something told me there had to be another narrative. I changed my search engine to Brave search and Yandex, and then as if by magic a whole new paradigm appeared before my eyes. There was a lot of independent research and journalism, most of which referenced a book named 'Dissolving Illusions – Suzanne Humphries', I'd recommend that everyone read this book (15). The book looks back at the history of poverty in the western world and links the end of poverty with the decline of infectious disease. They also added the beginning of vaccination /immunization to their poverty data. From their data it was apparent that nearly all infectious disease had dropped by 90% or more pre 1950 when no antibiotics and the majority of immunizations weren't available. The real saviour of infectious disease was actually sanitary improvement's, nutritional improvements, frozen and refrigerated food, flushing toilet systems, clean drinking water and safeguarding against childhood labour, incidentally all becoming the norm in society at the exact same time infectious disease significantly dropped. By the way all their data is verifiable and pulled from the Vital statistics from the UK and US which produce identical graphs, incredibly they've known this data since at least 1960.

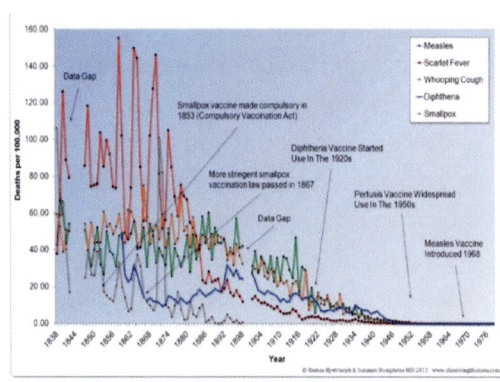

England and Wales mortality rates from various infectious diseases from 1838 to 1978. (Record of mortality in England and Wales for 95 years as provided by the Office of National Statistics, published 1997; Report to The Honourable Sir George Cornewall Lewis, Bart, MP, Her Majesty's Principal Secretary of State for the Home Department, June 30, 1860, pp. a4, 205; Essay on Vaccination by Charles T. Pearce, MD, Member of the Royal College of Surgeons of England; Parliamentary Papers, the 62nd Annual Return of the Registrar General 1899 (1891–1898))

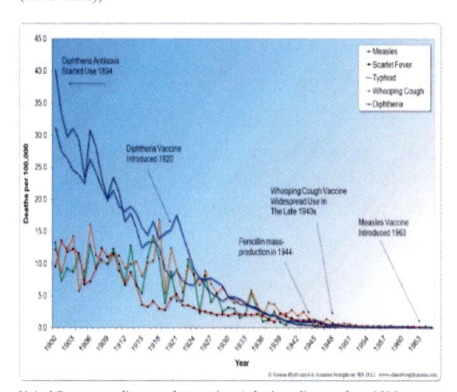

United States mortality rates from various infectious diseases from 1900 to 1965. (Vital Statistics of the United States 1937, 1938, 1943, 1944, 1949, 1960, 1967, 1976, 1987, 1992; Historical Statistics of the United States— Colonial Times to 1970 Part 1; Health, United States, 2004, US Department of Health and Human Services; Vital Records & Health Data Development Section, Michigan Department of Community Health; US Census Bureau, Statistical Abstract of the United States: 2003; Reported Cases and Deaths from Vaccine Pre-ventable Diseases, United States, 1950-2008)

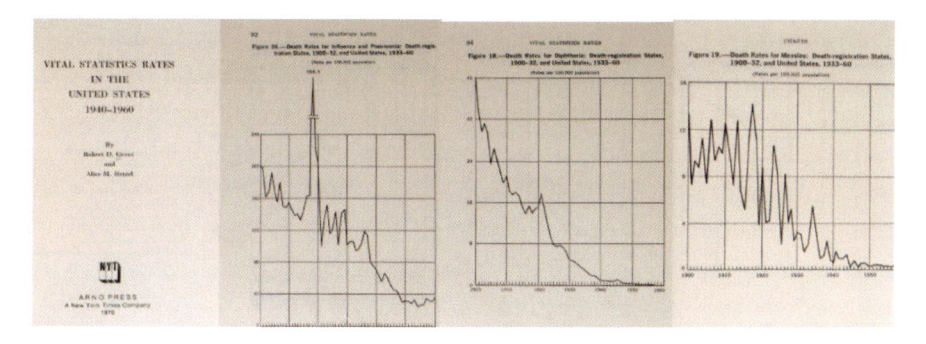

Reiterating their argument that vaccines had little impact in the decline of infectious disease they displayed their data of scarlet fever deaths, which show there was a 100% decline with no vaccination developed, it disappeared without a vaccine. They also showed that scurvy, once thought to be an infectious disease, now known to be a vitamin C deficiency, declined at the same rate as other infectious disease including measles, which by the way is linked to a vitamin A deficiency. In fact, measles deaths had already dropped by 99% before the introduction of the first weakened virus vaccine in 1968. Contrary to mainstream narrative flu infections had significantly dropped before the introduction on the first vaccine circa 1970. The flu vaccine made no impact, which begs the question why do most governments promote a yearly flu vaccine? I guess you could say money talks, but I think it could be even more nefarious. The weakened flu virus vaccine is one of the only vaccines that still contain thimerosal which contains mercury as an ingredient (16). These neurotoxins are added to vaccines as additives and to stimulate an immune response. The stupid thing is the flu vaccine uses the previous year's strain, thus, if you didn't contract the previous year's flu strain your likely to become ill from the vaccine, it has no benefits. Thimerosal has been removed from all childhood vaccines as it is one of the deadliest neurotoxins known to man, yet they want kids to get injected with this garbage yearly via the flu shot. Is it any wonder that neurological issues are at an all-time high in the most vulnerable, children and the elderly? Neurological issues such as autism and degenerative disease such as Alzheimer's are now at epidemic levels. Take away the mainstream political rhetoric and It's pretty obvious that being injected with multiple neurotoxins is going to cause you neurological issues, especially in developing and declining bodies. The mainstream will have you believe the amounts of neurotoxins such as mercury by way of thimerosal and aluminium phosphate are not large enough quantities to cause concern. What they fail to mention is that most children, especially in the US, receive up to 50 shots of these neurotoxins before the age of 3 and over 70 before they reach adulthood. These heavy metal neurotoxins aren't soluble in the body and can't be excreted. Vital organs such as the brain mistake mercury and aluminium for beneficial minerals such as magnesium. They accidently store these heavy metals in the brain, I'm sure you can guess the rest!

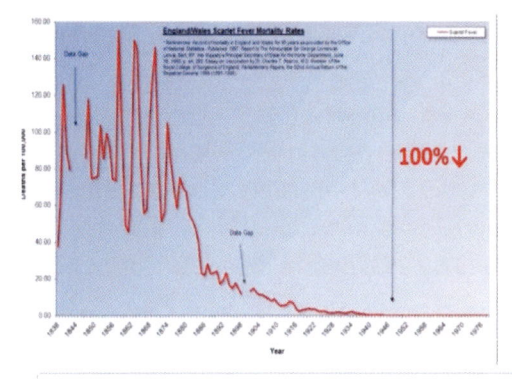

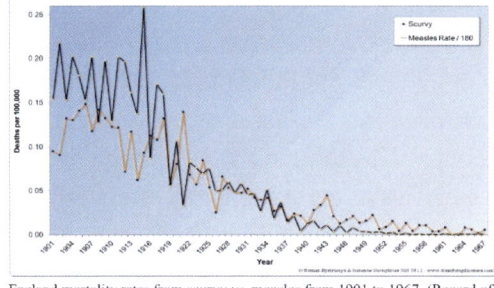

England mortality rates from scurvy vs. measles from 1901 to 1967. (Record of mortality in England and Wales for 95 years as provided by the Office of National Statistics, 1997)

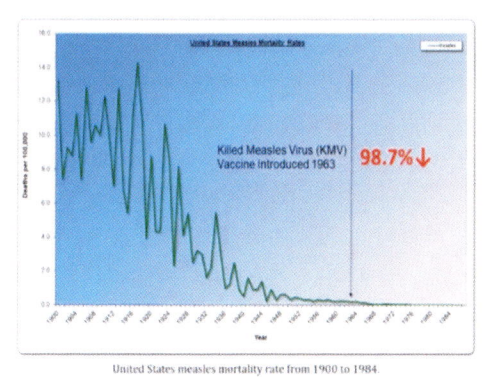

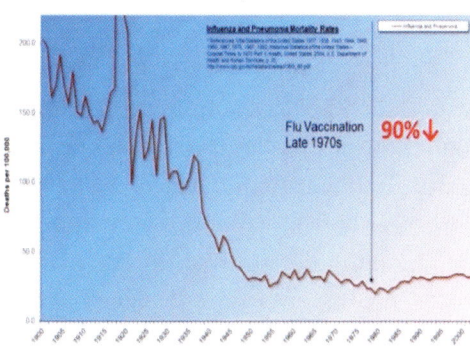

United States measles mortality rate from 1900 to 1984.

There are multiple studies highlighting another issue with multiple vaccination in a short period of time. Cumulative inactivated vaccine exposure that causes allergy development, highlighted from studies in Japan, who don't have a compulsory childhood vaccination schedule (17). There has also been shown to be strong correlation between childhood doctor visits and vaccination status, and I quote, the data indicate that unvaccinated children in the practice are not unhealthier than the vaccinated and indeed the overall results may indicate that the unvaccinated paediatric patients in this practice are healthier overall than the vaccinated (18).

One doctor took it upon himself to track allergies and neurological issues of this patients over a 10-year period. He found his vaccinated child patients suffered with a high rate of allergy induced issues as well as neurological issues including asthma, eczema, ADHD and many more. The unvaccinated children had a much lower rate of the same issues, some were even non-existent in the unvaccinated. What did he get by trying to publish his ground-breaking findings? He had his medical license suspended and later removed! You better not dare question their narrative! I know they say correlation doesn't guarantee causation but we now have multiple studies with the same outcome, you would think they would have more than enough reason for further research at the very least, but no, it gets shut down immediately in its tracks and is never considered for funding. From what I've seen, this seems to be the norm with findings outside of the mainstream narrative in all sciences, not just medicine (19).

Other infectious disease had uncanny correlation with lead arsenic-based pesticides and DDT. Polio was rife in the 1950's causing paralysis and we've all seen the horrific pictures of children on the iron lung machines. My father, a 50's child actually suffered with polio as a youngster, and the narrative was that due to vaccination they had the disease under control by the 1960's. The strange thing about polio was that it was a predominantly summer seasonal infection, as well as mainly effecting children. DDT once thought to be a safe chemical and an effective pesticide actually turned out to be a highly toxic poison and neurotoxin. DDT was sprayed on the streets; in the summer they sprayed children in outdoor pools and at the beach. Polio is linked to a degeneration of the spinal column nerves, from poisoning by several pesticides such as lead arsenate and DDT, which were in widespread use during outbreaks of Polio. However, Polio declined parallel to the decline of the usage of DDT (20). So, the question is, was polio an infectious disease or lead arsenic poisoning? Both of which have identical symptoms.

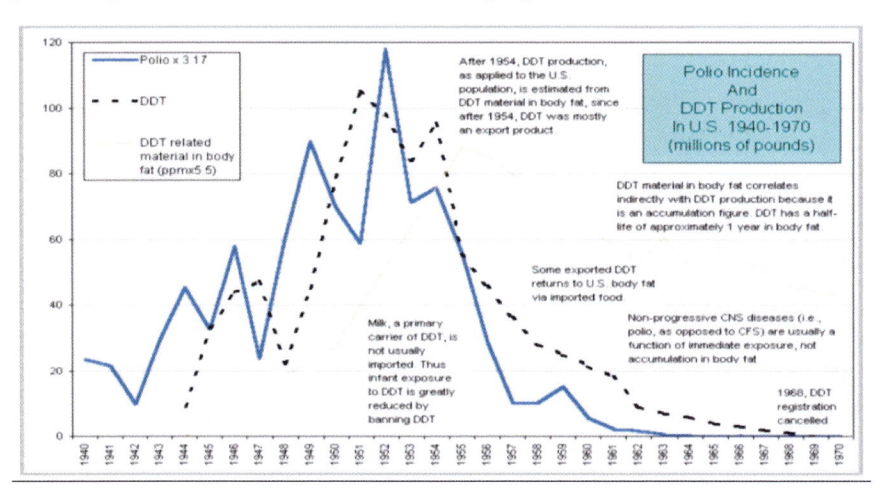

One of the earliest vaccines was developed for smallpox. In the early to mid-1800's the smallpox vaccine was mandated internationally. Now there is a history were not told about, back in those days there are documents that indicate there was a mass push back against this mandate, it was actually eerily similar to the covid malarky. There were anti-vaccination leagues on both sides of the Atlantic. There was regular demonstration on the safety and efficacy of the vaccines. Mothers were blaming the vaccine for injury and deaths of their children and huge amounts of children were still getting infected even after mass inoculation (21). Sounds very familiar! The people of Leicestershire, incidentally my county of birth, actually put an end to the UK mandate due to regular mass protest. Back then the media even dared to report on vaccine death and injury.

## "FAKE" POLIO VACCINE MAY KILL YOUR CHILD!!

INOCULATION FOR IMMUNITY IS STRICTLY A "THEORY" AND THE PRACTICE OF INOCULATION MAKES THE BODY "UNCLEAN" AND SUBJECT TO SICKNESS WHICH MAY BE POLIO.

About February first, there will begin in this country, the most horrible, unthinkable, dangerous, vicious crusade against HEALTH ever conceived. One million little children will be offered as sacrifices on the altar of greed . . . having their life's blood "polluted" with Dr. Salk's fraudulent vaccine . . . dead virus "pickled" in formalin, (formaldehyde) . . . embalming fluid if you please. This vaccination FRAUD is a frantic effort by the boon-doggling, charity brokers to prevent the public from learning the TRUTH about the UTTER WORTHLESSNESS of The March of Dimes.

ISN'T IT FACT . . . that Dr. Salk himself stated that after he had injected his serum into "test" children that he couldn't sleep for a few nights? Sickening . . . isn't it?? . . . Yet, he wants to use your child as a "human guinea-pig."

In Los Angeles, after a wide spread and intensive vaccination campaign was waged, according to Dr. Dale, County Epidemiologist, estimates there were approximately 4,000 CASES OF POLIO JUST ONE MONTH AFTER THE VACCINATION CAMPAIGN as compared with only 14 CASES the YEAR BEFORE.

rate running in places to almost 70% says, If the record of vaccination in the Philippines were ever to become a matter of general knowledge it would FINISH vaccination.

In the Philippines in a period of three years following compulsory vaccination, occurred the greatest smallpox epidemic in Philippine history . . . with 162,503 cases and 71,453 deaths. In 1918, 47,369 of those vaccinated came down with Smallpox . . . 16,477 DIED. In 1919 . . . 65,180 were stricken with Smallpox . . . 44,408 DIED.

There is one last interesting fact I discovered regarding vaccines, countries today that have a high vaccine uptake still have high infection rates. In communist China for example, they are very strict and mandate all vaccines. Even with a 99% vaccine uptake they still have huge numbers of deaths and infections. Could this be, that like in all communist countries, most of the population live in squalor and poverty? This finding aligns with the end of poverty being the saviour of endemic infectious disease narrative and not, as were indoctrinated to believe, vaccines.

However, this doesn't explain the WHO's reported high rates of measles in some countries with very high vaccination rates, such as China's which has a 99% vaccine uptake[46].

| Region | Member State | ISO country code | Total suspected measles cases | Total confirmed measles cases | Lab confirmed | EPI link | Clinically confirmed | Annualized measles incidence per 100'000 total population | Annualized discarded measles cases per 100'000 total population |
|---|---|---|---|---|---|---|---|---|---|
| SEAR | Indonesia | IDN | 12689 | 7928 | 1041 | 737 | 6150 | 3.14 | 1.88 |
| SEAR | Maldives | MDV | 0 | -9 | 0 | 0 | -9 | -2.56 | 2.56 |
| SEAR | Myanmar | MMR | 463 | 108 | 6 | 102 | 0 | 0.20 | 0.66 |
| SEAR | Nepal | NPL | 348 | 105 | 7 | 0 | 98 | 0.37 | 0.86 |
| SEAR | Sri Lanka | LKA | 3061 | 2488 | 1560 | 0 | 928 | 11.60 | 2.67 |
| SEAR | Thailand | THA | 1191 | 834 | 70 | 0 | 764 | 1.24 | 0.53 |
| SEAR | Timor-Leste | TLS | 80 | 52 | 25 | 20 | 7 | 4.51 | 2.43 |
| WPR | Australia | AUS | 335 | 335 | 317 | 18 |  | 1.42 | 0.00 |
| WPR | Brunei Darussalam | BRN | 16 | 0 |  |  |  | 0.00 | 3.78 |
| WPR | Cambodia | KHM | 636 | 0 |  |  |  | 0.00 | 4.13 |
| WPR | China | CHN | 112483 | 52485 | 47983 | 140 | 4362 | 3.77 | 4.30 |

If it's questionable that vaccines had the huge impact on the health of society that we're told then why do they continually push more vaccines on the population? The US which has the largest childhood vaccination schedule is one of the sickest nations on Earth while being one of the richest, least impoverished and also spending the most on pharmaceuticals. Isn't it strange that the US is the 44th placed nation in terms of chronic illness, right alongside Vietnam? As with covid vaccination it would seem most vaccines aren't safe or effective. The covid vaccine safe and effective line is provable propaganda only latched onto by the usual slave minded normies. How did they know it was safe and effective when they didn't have any long-term data? Many high figure health officials initially stated that transmission ends with the vaccinated (V4). How did they know early on that it stopped transmission when they didn't test for transmission before release? This was stated recently by a Pfizer employee who told the European court, and I quote, they didn't have time to test for transmission as they were moving at 'the speed of science', whatever that means!? (V5). When they realised it didn't stop transmission, they switched narratives to it prevents hospitalisations and deaths, how did they know this when there have, to my knowledge, been no randomised controlled studies on vaccinated and unvaccinated and of severity of symptoms, again provable propaganda!

If you think about it logically without the clown world narrative, wouldn't it be better for children today to get infected? These diseases nowadays have an almost non-existent infection fatality rate and natural immunity is far more robust that vaccine immunity, which is questionable anyway. That way you don't put kids at risk with neurotoxins and they also develop a robust immune system. Seems logical to me, but then again what other medication can the pharmaceutical companies sell to governments that their entire population have to take, multiple times? Vaccines are a pharmaceutical companies wet dream, not only do they have to be taken multiple times by the entire population but they also receive indemnity from courts for any injury or death claims. Thanks to the 1986 childhood vaccination act 1986 (22), these companies are not liable by law, the bill is left for the tax payers to pick up, it's all win, win. These companies' apparent greed reaches no boundaries, recently they've added a Hepatitis B vaccine for all babies, the sexually transmitted disease. They've also added a cervical cancer shot to every Childs schedule, that's right, boys being shot repeatedly for cervical cancer? It's almost like they just want to sell as many vaccines as possible!

An overview of data from the previous chapter can be viewed at the Annual Summary of Vital Statistics of the 20th century (23).

# 2019 CHILDHOOD VACCINE SCHEDULE

| 1962 | 1983 | 2019 | | | | |
|---|---|---|---|---|---|---|
| OPV | DTP (2 months) | Influenza (pregnancy) | Hep B (6 months) | Influenza (18 months) | Influenza (10 years) |
| Smallpox | OPV (2 months) | Tdap (pregnancy) | Rotavirus (6 months) | Hep A (18 months) | HPV (10 years) |
| DTP | DTP (4 months) | Hep B (birth) | DTaP (6 months) | Influenza (30 months) | Influenza (11 years) |
| 5 Doses | OPV (4 months) | Hep B (2 months) | HIB (6 months) | Influenza (42 months) | HPV (11 years) |
| | DTP (6 months) | Rotavirus (2 months) | PCV (6 months) | DTaP (4 years) | Tdap (12 years) |
| | MMR (15 months) | DTaP (2 months) | IPV (6 months) | IPV (4 years) | Influenza (12 years) |
| | DTP (18 months) | HIB (2 months) | Influenza (6 months) | MMR (4 years) | Meningococcal (12 years) |
| | OPV (18 months) | PCV (2 months) | Influenza (7 months) | Varicella (4 years) | Influenza (13 years) |
| | DTP (4 years) | IPV (2 months) | HIB (12 months) | Influenza (5 years) | Influenza (14 years) |
| | OPV (4 years) | Rotavirus (4 months) | PCV (12 months) | Influenza (6 years) | Influenza (15 years) |
| | Td (15 years) | DTaP (4 months) | MMR (12 months) | Influenza (7 years) | Influenza (16 years) |
| | 24 Doses | HIB (4 months) | Varicella (12 months) | Influenza (8 years) | Meningococcal (16 years) |
| | | PCV (4 months) | Hep A (12 months) | Influenza (9 years) | Influenza (17 years) |
| | | IPV (4 months) | DTaP (18 months) | HPV (9 years) | Influenza (18 years) |
| | | | | | 72 Doses |

## WHAT HAPPENED IN 1986?

- In 1986, Reagan passed a law that gave legal immunity to vaccine manufacturers.
- They could no longer be sued for injuries or death caused by their products. Safe vaccines wouldn't need such protection.
- Once that law passed, we suddenly 'needed' 48 additional doses of vaccines. (Do you remember any outbreaks in 1989?)
- Also, since that law was passed, U.S. Federal Government has paid out more than $4 Billion in vaccine injury compensation, and that's only a fraction of actual injuries.
- The U.S. gives more vaccines than most developed countries, yet we have the sickest kids

## GUESS WHAT?

The CDC has only ever tested MMR and Thimerosal for a link to autism. The remaining 15 vaccines and 37 common ingredients remain untested for links to autism.

**INFORMED CHOICE USA**
CONSUMER ADVOCACY | EDUCATION | EMPOWERMENT

For more information and sources, please visit www.InformedChoiceUSA.org

**THERE ARE RISKS | YOU HAVE CHOICES**

## Chapter 3 – Casedemic, Masks & Cults

Governments of the G7 nations announced a PCR covid test was now available for public use. In the UK they were free to order on the NHS website, this amounted to £3 billion a day at the cost of the tax paying public, this was on top of billions already paid out for furlough to incentivise staying at home and keeping your business closed. Your average normie thought this was a great incentive, free money with no consequences, or so they thought. During the height of the first covid wave back when I was collecting covid tests, I was collecting on average around 20 per day that was in the whole of East Devon. Now the tests were free, I was collection around 50 from each post box in the small town where I worked. Simultaneously I had noticed the UK media reporting a huge spike in cases, my initial reaction was how can they compare the first wave with only hospital and a few public tests with a mass public test rollout? It was obvious to me that testing had increased dramatically yet they were comparing cases during a time with limited testing. Before the mass public testing began, I had already noticed a mass push in regards to case reporting in the media, you could literally type any number from 1-1000 and covid cases in the search bar and search results would display a completely separate story for any and every number, bizarre! What was stranger was that most stories came from MSNBC news, a Microsoft corporation, Mr Gates again. It definitely felt they were planting the seed for things to come. My brother stated on Facebook, in true ignorant normie fashion that this was completely normal and to be expected and that anyone questioning the pandemic, even by providing their own data, was a psychopath. Unfortunately for him, he obviously naively believes everyone has the same morals and values as him and that tyranny of the rich and powerful was something confined to the past. The truth is that YOU wouldn't do anything to hurt the public but THEY would, I believe the elites think of the public as nothing more than cattle. At this point I was becoming increasingly disillusioned with Facebook or commie book as I now refer to it with its single narrative shit show of censorship. I foresaw the direction Facebook was headed and permanently deleted my account which I had held for 13 years, I can't tell you how good it feels not having to read brain dead normie perception and people defending their own enslavement, in fact I'd advise deleting all media developed by the META group, this is Facebook, Instagram and WhatsApp. At this point I started using twitter which seemed to have a far more intelligent user base, with people sharing hard science and far more logical debate, at last some based people that I can relate to, I can't tell you the number of times I questioned my own sanity before finding Twitter there are still droves of indoctrinated normies and trolls but at least it was more balanced than the META platforms. I believe the best way to differentiate a normie from a based person is the fact the normie doesn't question their own beliefs, logic or sanity. Whereas a based person question everything constantly. Normies seem to make up silly arguments and excuses against certain subjects to put their mind at rest rather than questioning every fine detail, they definitely prefer a comforting lie rather than admitting harsh truths. Thomas Sowell, one of my favourite economists once said "it is usually futile to try and talk facts and analysis to people who are enjoying a sense of moral superiority in their ignorance" in my mind ignorance is bliss but pure arrogance is actually collusion.

PCR tests had now become free at our office, I took one home and used clementine juice that I squeezed onto the test strip, it came back positive! At this point I thought I better take a closer look at the PCR test. My manager had tried to make it compulsory that everyone entering the building take a PCR test, having thought this was nonsensical given I was in peak health and walking 12 miles a day with 30Kg loads! I told him I would either not use the test if I was healthy or I'd go home at his discretion, which would mean on full pay. He then told me not to worry about testing!

Having worked for months with no testing and nobody going sick through the peak of the first wave of covid, now my colleges were off sick with covid left right and centre, I believe one college was off 5 times with covid over around a 6-month period, completely impossible I'm sure, given the robustness of natural immunity. Although it highlighted the PCR tests observable flaws. Nobody seemed to notice these obvious flaws and had no time for me explaining how flawed these tests were.  Some of my good friends at work tested positive, most of them experienced no symptoms and a couple said they experienced light cold like symptoms and were fine after a day or two. Nothing like the deadly disease you were led to believe on the national news. As cases increased it became apparent the death spike was not as significant as the initial wave. In the UK they made a PCR test compulsory for everyone entering hospital, which obviously included everyone in late stages of a terminal illness and with life threatening injury. Anyone who then came back with a positive test result was labelled a covid death if they had passed away within 28 days of a positive covid test, even if they had no covid symptoms! Crazy! Imagine how many people would have died of covid 28 days after brushing their teeth? An illogical policy but a great way to ensure a manipulated increase in covid deaths with skewed data. It gets worse, hospitals had been incentivised to label any death as covid by granting the hospital upwards of £30,000 per covid patient death. There was also another payment to hospitals for putting covid patients on a ventilator machine along with a dose of Midazolam in the UK and Remdesivir in the US. Both drugs known to cause kidney failure and potentially flood the lungs being a respiratory depressant. Make of that what you will (V6).  It should be noted that these drugs cost upwards of £2000 per dose, unlike vilified and demonised drugs such as Ivermectin which incidentally have no patent and cost pennies per dose.

In the UK and The US depending on which state/county you were in the PCR tests were used at a threshold between 35 and 45 cycles. Each cycle is a factor of the next not a multiple, by the time you reach 45 cycles you are getting to a magnification into the trillions. French researcher Didier Raoult had previously shown that a with a PCR cycle threshold of 35, no sample remained positive of infectious in cell culture (24). On further inspection it would seem that the PCR test was never previously used for establishing infections, it had been developed by Nobel Prize winning biochemist Kerry Mullis who described the PCR as an important tool for crime scene investigation and for forensics, he also stated that the PCR should not be used for disease as it can pick up nearly anything and make it look like a bunch of something, at such magnification it would be impossible to say for certain if someone was infectious or not (V7). Kerry Mullis was said to be a healthy 70-year-old and keen surfer before he died, just months before the covid pandemic, quite a coincidence given he would have no doubt been a load advocate and voice against the use of the PCR to determine infectious disease. He was also not a fan of the notorious Dr Fauci, especially his conduct during the AIDS pandemic in the 1980's. He stated Fauci was a pure administrative scientist and shouldn't be in the position that he's in (V8).

What was becoming apparent as time went on was that this was a casedemic not really a pandemic; people started referring to the pandemic as plandemic, a name far more suitable. The media, news and government were pushing the case scaremongering with everything they could. You had updates on the radio, newspapers, case counters on the news. The aim was clearly to scare the population into submission and gain public support for their tyrannical policy change. In true Orwellian fashion it became apparent that governments had changed the definition of pandemic, previously for a pandemic to be declared the excess death would need to reach 5x average levels. Under its new definition the WHO could declare a pandemic whenever they saw fit, solely at their digression. It should be noted that many definitions were changed to suit the narrative during the clown world years. We saw changes in pandemic, immunity, vaccines, believe it or not we even had a change in the definition of a Woman, this will be covered more later on...

During the hearing Wodarg testified the WHO, then under China's director-general Margaret Chan (2007-2017), deliberately changed the definition for a pandemic and downgraded its criteria in order to make it easier to declare one.

The old definition used as an international standard was: "An influenza pandemic is a worldwide epidemic caused by a new strain of virus which leads to infection rates and mortality rates which exceed seasonal but similarly heavy waves of influenza by several orders of magnitude. A precondition for an influenza pandemic is the appearance of a viral subtype which had not yet circulated amongst the human population or which had occurred so long ago that no residual immunity remains amongst the population, and which is capable of provoking severe illness and of disseminating effectively from one human to another."

The new definition downgraded the criteria to stating simply that there had to be a virus that spread beyond borders to which people had no immunity. As such a pandemic no longer has to *exceed seasonal and heavy waves of influenza by several orders of magnitude*, and can be much milder than the seasonal flu — which again has the mortality burden of up to half a million annually.

As Dr. Ulrich Keil testified, the *severity* of the disease was no longer relevant to declare a pandemic. When he asked Dr. Krause from the Robert Koch Institute in Berlin "What might happen if WHO next year defined sneezing as a pandemic. Would you also start a vaccination campaign?" Dr. Krause "responded with a clear YES!"

---

**World Health Organization**

Home / Newsroom / Q&A Detail /
Coronavirus disease (COVID-19): Serology

### Coronavirus disease (COVID-19): Serology

9 June 2020 | Q&A

**What is herd immunity?**

Herd immunity is the indirect protection from an infectious disease that happens when a population is immune either through vaccination or immunity developed through previous infection. This means that even people who haven't been infected, or in whom an infection hasn't triggered an immune response, they are protected because people around them who are immune can act as buffers between them and an infected person. The threshold for establishing herd immunity for COVID-19 is not yet clear.

---

**World Health Organization**

Home / Newsroom / Q&A Detail /
Coronavirus disease (COVID-19): Serology, antibodies and immunity

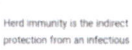

### Coronavirus disease (COVID-19): Serology, antibodies and immunity

13 November 2020 | Q&A

**What is herd immunity?**

'Herd immunity', also known as 'population immunity', is a concept used for vaccination, in which a population can be protected from a certain virus if a threshold of vaccination is reached.

Herd immunity is achieved by protecting people from a virus, not by exposing them to it. Read the Director-General's *12 October media briefing speech* for more detail.

Vaccination (pre-2015): Injection of a killed or weakened infectious organism in order to <u>prevent</u> the disease.

Vaccination (2015-2021): The act of introducing a vaccine into the body to produce <u>immunity</u> to a specific disease.

Vaccination (Sept 2021): The act of introducing a vaccine into the body to produce <u>protection</u> from a specific disease.

"TITLE XXI. —VACCINES
"Subtitle 1. —National Vaccine Program
"ESTABLISHMENT
"SEC. 2101. The Secretary shall establish in the Department of Health and Human Services a National Vaccine Program to achieve <u>optimal prevention of human infectious diseases</u> through immunization and to achieve optimal prevention against adverse reactions to vaccines. The Program shall be administered by a Director selected by the Secretary.

The CDC changed the definition of "Vaccine" but that doesn't change the U.S. Law Public Law 99-660 (The Reagan Pharma sell-out in 1986 courtesy of Henry Waxman's corruption)

The rise in cases enabled the government to implement some nonsensical policies. First off, we had the introduction of mask mandates in indoor settings, in some countries even outside. China, Australia and Canada being the worst affected by tyrannical authoritarian policy. China was to be expected given their communist history, Australia and Canada on the other hand were seen to be great nations for free, easy going living, yet they quickly turned into dystopian hell holes. As I stated before we weren't required to wear masks in our office for 7 months before they mandated indoor masking in line with government policy change. I was the only person who questioned this nonsensical change in our office, all the other normies masked up no questions asked, even after 7 months of everyone being absolutely fine mask less previously during the height of the pandemic. Eventually, I begrudgingly agreed to a plastic face shield, the ones with gaps around your whole face, but as long as my managers thought it was ideal protection against virus particles then I was happy to oblige with their clown world logic and remain virtually unmasked. The only time I wore a mask at all was when I had to buy food.

You've all seen pictures of biologists working in contaminated areas, they're full hazmat suited and sealed air tight, the idea that a piece of cloth can't be penetrated by virus particles is a logical fallacy. Policemen though thought it necessary to arrest and physically abuse anyone who dared to remain unmasked, some shocking footage emerged from Australia, this abuse was said to be for their own safety? (V9).

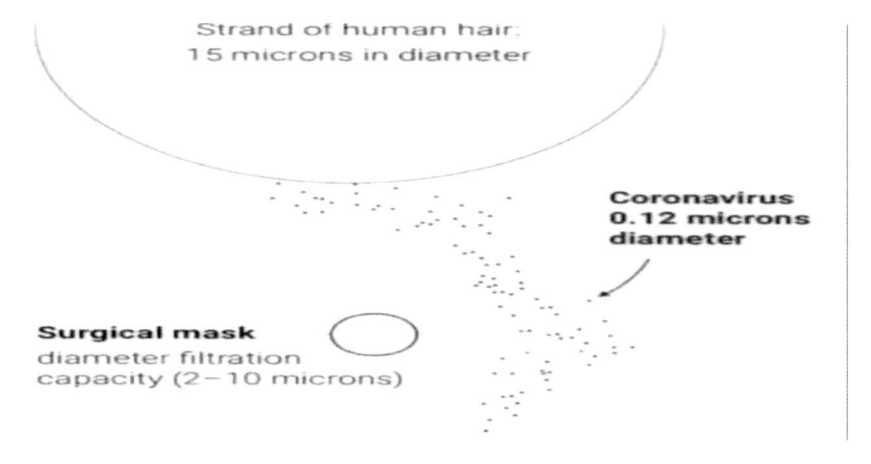

Strand of human hair: 15 microns in diameter

Coronavirus 0.12 microns diameter

Surgical mask diameter filtration capacity (2–10 microns)

Previous studies all pointed to surgical masks being insignificant in terms of virus protection, masks are commonly used by surgeons to prevent open wounds becoming infected. People in Asia are known to wear masks although it is more of a cultural common curtsey if someone is ill rather than scientifically viable. Leading health authority figures in the UK and elsewhere initially stated that

Masking was not necessary and it could even have a detrimental effect by way of unnecessary touching of the mask and the face potentially spreading more bacteria (V10). Then all of a sudden, all governments did a 180-degree change in policy making masks mandated. Call me cynical but like with lockdowns it would seem the government were testing obedience levels to policy, when they realised people wanted more lockdowns and were wearing masks anyway without the mandate then they started changing the goal posts to see what they could get away with. I have heard excuses such as the government had to be seen to do something even if it wasn't effective. I had seen a News night episode that said the WHO didn't recommend masking that was until they received political lobbying, then they changed their mind (V11). The best clown world narrative I heard was that they didn't want nurses to go without masks so they lied to the public to prevent a mass public purchase, the same way they had previously with toilet paper, sounds like bullshit to me especially with all the footage of empty hospitals and nurses with nothing better to do than TikTok dances (V12). During that period, I continually spoke to my ex's mother who worked in the Torbay hospital, every time I asked what the covid ward was like she said empty. Bearing in mind Torbay had the supposed first case of covid so the idea that the virus hadn't reached this area, as some normies had suggested, made no sense as per normie logic, anything to put their mind at rest (25). Every time I drove past the nightingale hospital at Sowton in Exeter it seemed derelict, not a sole in sight and it always had an empty car park (V13). Even with all this non observable pandemic all the brain dead normies followed orders to bang pans outside their doors at 8pm every Thursday, much to my disgust, I remember walking along taking my dog for a walk think Jesus this has to be the peak of the clown world, this had to be the epitome of the group think normie, unfortunately not! (V14).

As winter progressed the cognitive dissonance of the mask cult people became more evident. You regularly saw people alone in their cars masked up, sometimes with a double mask and a face shield for good measure. The general clown world consensus was that if you're not masking then you're not a good person and you're putting others at danger. The fact that they did absolutely nothing didn't seem to matter as long as you were seen to be doing your bit of virtue signalling and unquestionably adhered to the groupthink clown world logic. It doesn't take a lot of critical thinking to come to the conclusion that if someone is masked that by their clown world logic, they are now safe. So how can someone who isn't sick and doesn't want to wear a mask be a threat to a masked up normie who thinks his mask is the perfect protection? As you can see, their normie logic exposes their own normie argument! They also used the same logic for the vaccinated. The normies proudly exclaiming that they were vaccinated and they had done the right thing (even though they didn't need it). Then tried to demonise the unvaccinated for putting the vaccinated at risk. So, lets get this straight, the vaccinated were safe because they're vaccinated but the unvaccinated are putting the vaccinated, who are now safe because of the vaccine, in danger??? This satire perfectly reflects their clown world logic at the time (V15).

It was truly a disturbing time in history when this thought process went mainstream and infected their heads like a mass formation psychosis. Most of Europe had spiralled into a two-tier society, the unvaccinated not being able to join the rest of society. The historically fascist countries fared worst, Italy, Germany and in Austria they weren't even allowed to leave their homes. You could say fascist ideology didn't go away; it was just shut down until it had another opportunity to arise. Australia and Canada were also particularly authoritarian and using non-scientific precautions against the unvaccinated. At this time, I had work colleges stating it was our fault (unvaccinated people) that lockdown was continuing and that we were selfish, they had no idea that it was their doublethink, obedience and lack of understanding that was causing them to turn into fascists with logic Hitler would have been proud off. I remember having an argument with an older work college who was very pro vax mandate and pompous, that day I was working in the office so decided to print off the latest scientific papers on transmission regarding covid vaccines, they were finding no difference in the viral load of vaccinated or unvaccinated (26). Also, an article in the Lancet which stated the stigmatisation of the unvaccinated was unjust and unscientific, they also stated it was a slippery path to go down given previous stigmatisation of minority groups most notably for religious beliefs in

Europe circa 1940 and race in the United States (27). I left it at his desk to read, highlighting the relevant sections, funnily enough he never came back to me regarding the subject.

I had never understood how a population could be coerced and be perpetrators during times such as the Nazi era, but now I think I do. Most of the average population are the perpetrators, a handful of elites can't orchestrate their tyranny without a population that acquiesce. Sure, you'd think you'd have saved Ann Frank, in reality you would have complied and probably turned her in given the opportunity. What people don't understand is that Hitler was democratically elected into power and his ideology and policy was accepted by the population and the academics of the time. A lesson should be learnt by the current day radical left enthusiasts, look at what happened the last time a population and government dabbled in radical ideology, looking back at history it should be apparent to everyone that legality is not morality.

Back to the mask cult, not only were all pre pandemic scientific papers finding masks had no significant effect against virus particles or influenza transmission, now we had real world data from around the globe, guess what, surprise, surprise, it found no difference in infection rate masked mandates and unmasked nations and states. In Austria they went to the extent to mandate N95 masks but again there was no difference in infection rates, in fact Austria had some of the highest infection rates in Europe. Like lockdowns which failed to prevent deaths, masks failed to prevent infections. At best you could say these measures prolonged deaths and infections but didn't decrease them at all. Given this knowledge, some nations still regularly threaten lockdowns and mask mandates when they announce spikes in covid cases, could this covid malarky be dare I say it, political and not scientific. If it's not nefarious central planning then it's definitely circular logic whereby each time more extreme measures are supposedly needed due to things getting worse, they lead to a worse outcome, therefore they need stricter more extreme measures, and we continually go around and around in a perpetual cycle of tyranny. It should be noted that some of the studies coming out of the NIIH and CDC regarding mask effectiveness are borderline comical, they have a handful of participants and no controls, I was also shocked to find that the while premise of the asymptomatic spread as a driver of the covid pandemic was based from a study with a handful of participants, it was said a hairdresser passed on covid to 16 of her customers, that's settled then! (28). A breakdown of all the science and real-world data regarding masks can be found here at the next reference (29).

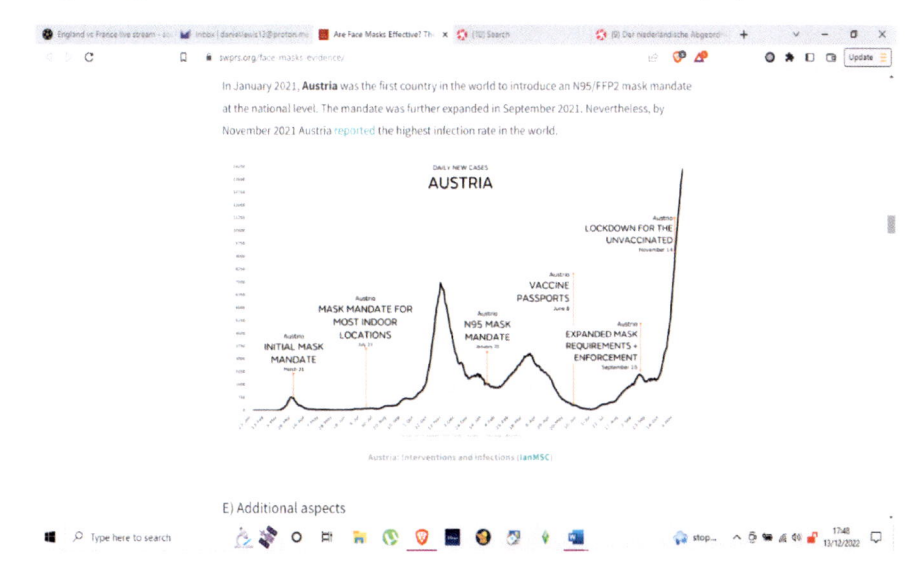

E) Additional aspects

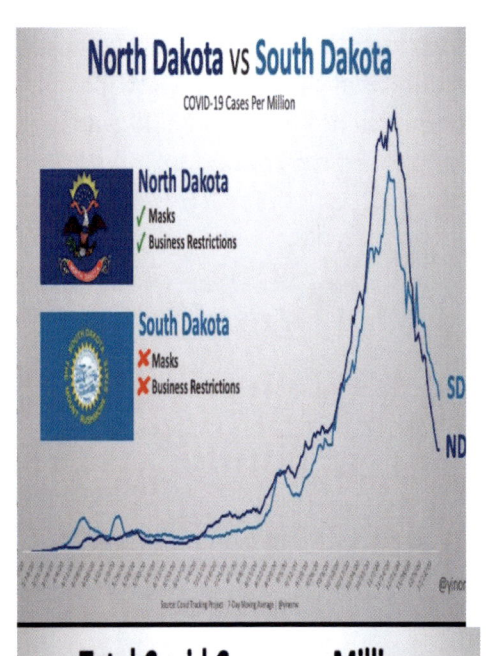

## North Dakota vs South Dakota
COVID-19 Cases Per Million

**North Dakota**
- ✓ Masks
- ✓ Business Restrictions

**South Dakota**
- ✗ Masks
- ✗ Business Restrictions

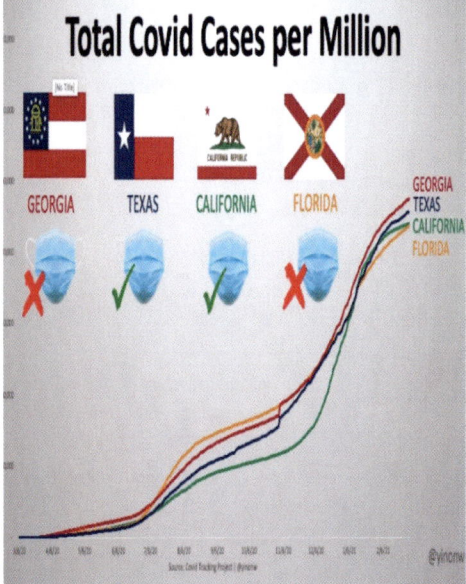

## Total Covid Cases per Million

GEORGIA ✗
TEXAS ✓
CALIFORNIA ✓
FLORIDA ✗

# Chapter 4 – Clown World Policy & Politically Correct Wokeness

Before 2016 I had little to know interest in politics, I couldn't relate to any politicians, they all seemed like toffs who had no idea about day-to-day life. I suppose you could have called me left of centre regarding my personal views, like most young people trying to find the way up the ladder in society. With no real assets other than my house I had to reason to align with conservative ideas and I'd never studied politics or economics to any degree. I guess the left leaning rhetoric is pushed on you at school, this is more clearly evident today. Nowadays It seems that anyone who doesn't agree with the extreme left-wing ideology is now considered far right, which is now used as a derogatory term, instead of merely someone with opposing ideas and political views. Just five years ago I'd have been considered left wing, now my opinions would have me ladled a right-wing extremist, this is how far and how fast the left wing woke agenda travelled over a relatively short period of time. In my opinion the woke agenda is the epitome of the clown world and incidentally rose to prominence at around the same time as the clown world began. It's pretty clear the media, social media, universities, the sciences, academia and schools all align with and are under control of the left, especially in the US. We'll delve into this deeper later on…

In 2016 I decided to make my first ever political vote (I was 35) I was going to vote for the UK to leave the EU during the Brexit referendum, at the time the only reason I needed was that it went against the Tory doctrine. David Cameron the then Prime minister had called a referendum as he was sure people wanted to remain in the EU. Results didn't go his way and he subsequently stepped down and resigned as prime minister. Only recently I became aware of the importance of Brexit in terms of the UK's independent sovereignty and not having to abide by fascists EU laws and regulations. Brexit is now blamed on a number of issues due to it going against the elite's world governance agenda, I believe they wanted us to remain in the EU and that's the reason for all the unpatriotic propaganda we receive to sway public opinion for the return to the EU. Normies never look at the bigger picture, they're always looking for something to pin the blame. So far, I've heard Brexit is the reason for inflation and the cost-of-living crisis, so it's nothing to do with out-of-control government money printing aka legal counterfeit, tyrannical lockdown policy and nonsensical net zero climate policy? I believe leaving the EU was the best possible outcome, it leaves the UK a sovereign nation not answerable to tyrannical EU and globalist policy.

Fast-forward to 2019 and there was a general election. At this time, we had Boris Johnson of the conservatives, who was using the slogan 'get Brexit done' for his political campaign. Hypocritical, given he was a stern critic of leaving the EU, I can remember thinking to myself "Why are people believing this buffoon? Surely, they can remember a couple of years ago when the conservatives wanted to remain in the EU?" people, especially normies seem to have incredibly short memories! Especially when it goes against their ideology and narrative.

In opposition was Jeremy Corbyn of the Labour party. To me Corbyn seemed like a genuine kind of politician with morals and I liked his ideas and policies he wanted to implement, especially publicising national services which were being run into the ground for crony capitalist profit. I had first-hand experience of witnessing Royal Mails demise from a fantastic efficient public service to a company only looking to make profit and failing miserably with customer quality satisfaction, in just a few short years into privatisation. For the first time in my life, I felt I could relate to a politician, I decided for the first time in my life I'd make the effort and get out and vote for Corbyn. Now that I'd made up my mind, I was voting for Corbyn, I was sure most would follow, after all how could they vote for Boris, a buffoon and the type of corrupt career politician who would take food from a baby given half a chance. The days following within my office it became apparent that most of the staff were voting for Boris, bearing in mind these are working class people voting right wing? Is there anything more stupid than voting for your own enslavement and voting to have your own working conditions slashed? Our CWU union even sent all staff a memo stating it was imperative that we vote Labour otherwise the company would be in serious trouble, as we see today, they weren't wrong.

I had noticed the memo made little to no effect in regards to my colleagues' opinions, the majority of them were still voting conservative. When I asked colleagues why they wouldn't consider a Corbyn vote, even after the CWU had stated it would be our downfall if we didn't, all I got was guys shouting out that he's an anti-Semite, he's a terrorist sympathiser, he's an IRA informant, he's anti-military scum. I would reply to their comments stating it would be unlikely he would be able to run for prime minister if any of those statements were true, and that he was actually a peace negotiator who had always stood for peace and against human rights violations such as the apartheid which he admirably opposed in the 80's. I might as well not have bothered, they didn't want to know, to my amazement I questioned one guy who stated Corbyn was an anti-Semite, I asked him why he thought Corbyn was anti-Semitic, it turned out he didn't even know what anti-Semitic meant and was just spurting out crap he'd read in the papers. I think this was the first time I became aware of political propaganda, and I couldn't believe everyone was falling for it even though they were going to impoverish themselves as a result. Looking back, I would say the media were compliant with the elite's agenda, Boris would be an easier character to manipulate, Corbyn on the other hand had morals and was anti-establishment, he would not be an easy individual to sway or manipulate, hence he got propagated into oblivion. The truth is, unfortunately a good way to establish if someone can change anything for the better is how demonised they are in the media. I now believe politics is merely to placate the population into thinking they have a choice, they don't, special interests always get what they want. Unless laws are changed political lobbying will always occur, politicians are bought and paid for by the elites and democracy, unfortunately is an illusion.

Fast-forward a couple of years and we had Donald Trump winning the presidency in the US. At the time I was pretty happy about this given Trump wasn't a career corrupt politician and already had wealth and power so probably wouldn't be as easily manipulated with political lobbying. It also became apparent that UK politics is a farce, they would never dream of going against the US, when was the last time the UK spoke out against one of the US proxy wars? Exactly! We're merely a US puppet or little brother who bows to our US masters at any opportunity. If any nation rejects the dollar for trade, they usually end up getting a good old dose of US freedom and democracy aka fire bombed and a US friendly government coup. See Sadam Hussein of Iraq and Mudafa Gadhafi of Libya for prime examples of what happens is you reject the dollar. Put it this way I don't think the US would have been bothered if their main national resources were broccoli.

Almost as soon as Trump came to power it became apparent that the media would do anything to get him out of office, I mean the propaganda was off the charts and the normies were lapping it up!

**Leftist during the Trump presidency**

*This is unbearable.*

**Leftist during the Biden presidency**

*THIS IS FINE.*

Trumps 2016 election win saw an instant rise in anti-Trump propaganda within the corporate media. Coincidently, this type of political propaganda was only matched by the 2018 Corbyn propaganda, it was mostly character assassination combined with anything the media could pin on Trump or even anything they could fabricate. The Russian collusion stories from early 2016 have since been found to be fraudulent; in fact they were a pure fabrication leaked to the press by various democrats, a hoax one could say. Like Corbyn it seems Trump wasn't going to go along with the elite deep state narrative, hence he was propagated into oblivion and still is even now two years after losing the presidency; they really don't want him to run for president in 2024! From what I can tell Trumps policies weren't at all that bad. The MAGA movement literally stands for make America great again, not a bad thing considering the States observable decline over the last decade. Trump is a populist, although obviously narcissistic and not everybody's cup of tea, I genuinely believe he wanted to do his best for America as a nation. He wanted to bring manufacturing and jobs back to the states which had previously been sold out to cheap foreign labour. During Trumps tenure he didn't invade another nation, he had peace talks with Putin of Russia and Kim Jong-un of North Korea, and although the media would have you believe he was trying to start World War 3. The media even tried to liken Trump to Hitler stating he was a fascist, a term used far too loosely these days, the average person calling someone a fascist probably can't even define it. If they could they'd know that Trump clearly isn't a fascist. Fascism is merely the merging of state and corporations, something that Trump didn't do as far as I'm aware. Fascist ideology actually aligns far more with the modern-day US left who are clearly merging with media and social media to censor any other political view, they are also merging with big pharma and large corporations making these companies insanely rich with their mandates and policy. The idea that fascism is confined to the right is a lie, historically it did arise with right wing leaders such as Mussolini and Stalin yet it can arise with any political ideology once it becomes radical, as we are seeing with the extreme left of today.

In 2020 we saw Trump lose the presidency to Joe Biden, the right was convinced of voter fraud, and for the first time I got a taste of the left's hypocrisy. In 2016 the left was convinced of voter fraud, but now the tides had turned they were proclaiming that the US voter system was one of the least vulnerable to voter fraud and that any suggestion of fraud should be seen as domestic terrorism. This is beyond the scope of this book but I would advise anyone to watch the documentary 2000 mules which cover this subject in detail (V16). Joe Biden seemed to have no policies; he simply campaigned with anti-Trump narratives. It seemed the left was so happy to get Trump out of office that they didn't care that Biden had no policies to note, was clearly declining mentally, was a career corrupt politician; only the Clinton crime family have a worse reputation than the Biden's. Not to mention Biden has a crack smoking son who lives off Daddies dodgy dealings with Ukrainian energy companies, 10% for the big guy! Obviously, all covered up by the media in the run up to the election, imagine the scenes had any of this been Trump! See the Twitter files for an overview of the collusion between big tech and the government running up to the 2020 election (20). Biden has made for some of the best gaffs since president Bush, if you want 5 minutes of hilarious gaffs can I point you to the following video (V17), I must warn you, it's hard to watch. Strangely enough in true clown world fashion the corporate press in America seem to pretend that Biden's obvious cognitive decline isn't happening. Biden is clearly the worst president in living memory, do you really think Biden is capable of making and decisions? The man can't string a coherent sentence together (V17a). But he's not alone, I'd say every president since Kennedy was placed into power to be easily manipulated by the deep state. The deep state are a group of wealthy elites and the CIA that make all the important decisions in the US in the shadows. This is the reason JFK was assassinated, he was going to end the federal reserve (V17b) and give power back to the people. It has since been released in a declassified document that JFK was murdered by the CIA, this was not surprisingly ignored in the media.

The left of today have become so far detached from reality that they favour radical theatrical ideology over observable truth and reality. The movement known as 'Woke' not to be confused with 'awake' is the epitome of the radical left ideology. The woke politicians and population want to believe that their woke agenda is being alert to prejudice and discrimination although one could argue that wokeness is the epitome of ignorant, a state of awareness only achieved by those ignorant enough to find injustice in everything apart from their own behaviour. It seems the woke agenda is latched onto by the snowflakes of society, they achieve moral status via victimhood. These people want to feel oppressed and love any opportunity to openly display their false virtue, Elon Musk expertly labelled wokeness as a mind virus and the ability to be nasty shielded by false virtue. You simply only need to speak to one of these woke individuals to find Elon is on point, they seem to always be a 'Karen' type of individual who would do anything to find faults in anyone and lacks the ability to critically think, the term that springs to mind is narcissist, I think you have to me a narcissist to some degree to align with the woke movement. The whole censorship agenda from the left is merely because their arguments are so weak and easily dismissed when challenged with reality, their only option is censorship to win a debate. They seem to be so entrenched with their radical ideology echo chamber that they think everyone thinks the same way, not only a fringe minority. One step outside of their echo chamber and they would find that the average Joe on the street thinks that most of their ideology is incoherent and insane nonsense. A prime example being gender ideology and infinite genders, completely insane!

If you're unaware of the radical left ideology you should start with the following-

- Gender ideology
- Critical race theory (BLM)
- Cancel culture
- Climate crisis

**Racist**
*noun*
A person who wins an argument with a Lefty

**Homophobe**
*noun*
A person who wins an argument with a Lefty

**Bigot**
*noun*
A person who wins an argument with a Lefty

**Fascist**
*noun*
A person who wins an argument with a Lefty

**Islamophobe**
*noun*
A person who wins an argument with a Lefty

**Nazi**
*noun*
A person who wins an argument with a Lefty

**Misogynist**
*noun*
A person who wins an argument with a Lefty

**Hitler**
*noun*
A person who wins an argument with a Lefty

It wont take long for anyone of sound mind to spot the massive flaws and insane hypocrisy of any of the lefts current ideology. Orwell really would have been proud of the level of double think the left has achieved. Here are some of the hypocrisies I've spotted while navigating around the left's stance on current events.

- They state they 'follow the science' and are factual yet find it acceptable to find infinite amounts of genders out of absolutely nowhere. Some even state the science agrees with them.

- They are pro vax mandate yet also my body my choice regarding abortion. Some even stating that vaccines save lives yet can't comprehend that infant euthanasia is murder in any other form i.e., homicide & adult euthanasia (V18).

- They state they are anti-fascist yet beg for media censorship and the merging of media and pharma with the government.

- They can't define a woman yet can say for sure that a trans woman is one.

- They state science is settled and negate the scientific process which is to hypothesise for further research.

- They state you can identify as anything that you want and insist you respect their pronouns yet expect you to identify and label yourself as CIS.

- They state gender is more about emotion and feelings than biology yet they promote gender reassignment surgery and body modification for minors.

- Instead of healthy debate they try and deter any dissenters by resorting to name calling and labelling anyone who disagrees with their ideology as racist, misogynist or trans phobic.

"I think I am, therefore I am"
~ 'Woke' Descartes

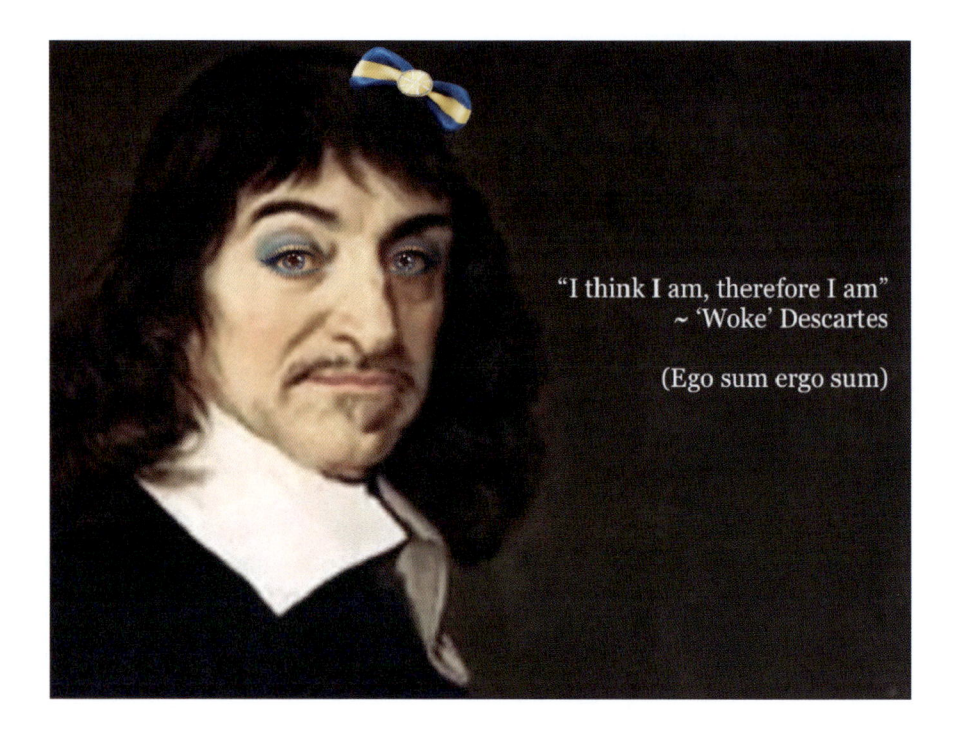

(Ego sum ergo sum)

The woke narcissists seem hell bent on pushing their junk science, most notably the climate crisis agenda. The woke left activists and politicians push their activism as settled science. Every couple of years they state the world will be in serious trouble in 10 years, then 10 years later nothing happens, then they repeat with a new prediction. I can remember at school in the early nineties that the agenda was that we were heading to an ice age, this was taught in my Geography classes. I believe it then turned to global warming circa 2000 and when it didn't get hotter they changed the name again, this time to climate change (no come back on that one). When the weather is colder than expected the media have jumped on the bandwagon and state cold weather is also man made climate change as well as isolated incidence of extreme weather, like its something new! There are high winds, storms and extreme hot and cold most years. More double think that Orwell would have been proud of!

The whole premise of the lefts climate crisis agenda is that the sun radiates on the carbon dioxide in the atmosphere and reflects back to the earth heating it up. What they fail to recognise is that CO2 is only 0.03% of the atmosphere; they totally negate the 78% nitrogen, 21% oxygen and 0.9% argon. They also fail to realise that CO2 is not a pollutant, its actually the element of life. The Earths current CO2 levels are at 400ppm, during the past the CO2 ppm has been 10x that amount while life has flourished, we are actually currently in a CO2 famine. The reason animals, plants and before that dinosaurs were so big was due to the high level of CO2 in the atmosphere. The most glaring over look of the left is that the climate has always changed naturally, we've had multiple ice ages and warm periods throughout recent history without any industrialisation, how did the cave men cause the medieval warm period and the little ice age? (30) The major issue with the climate model is that its mostly computer generated which is usually set to find the result you want rather than the reality and that they started measuring the temperature in 1850 which incidentally was the end of the little ice age and the coldest point in the last 10,000 years! (V19).

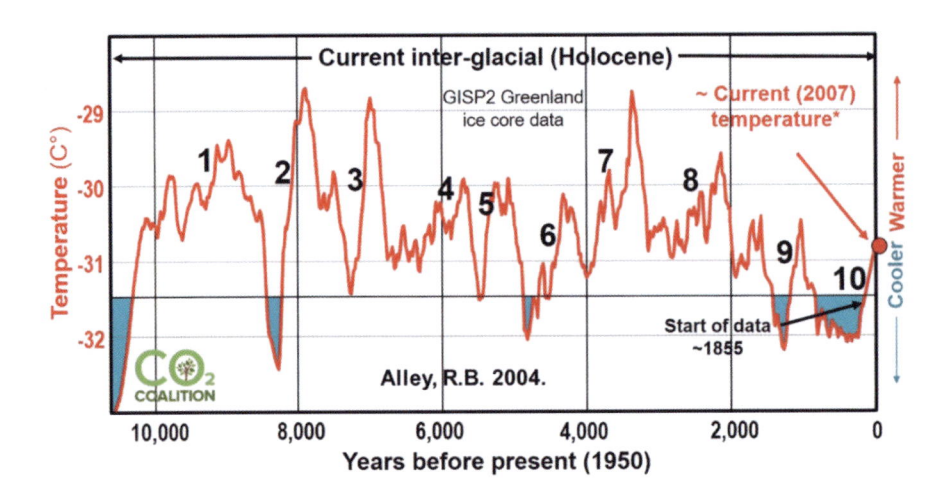

The general consensus is that 97% of climate scientists agree that manmade climate change is a crisis, one look into the consensus will show you that the data is skewed. What Mann et al did was state the majority of climate studies agree man causes climate change, what he failed to mention is that only 0.4% of the studies state man made industrialisation as a cause (31). Hotter climates are generally where humans have flourished, it's the cold weather which notoriously causes humans more issues. There are actually thousands of climate scientists who reject the climate crisis ideology most notably the most published climate scientist Judith Curry and before that David Bellamy was censored and banished from the BBC for questioning the climate crisis ideology (32).

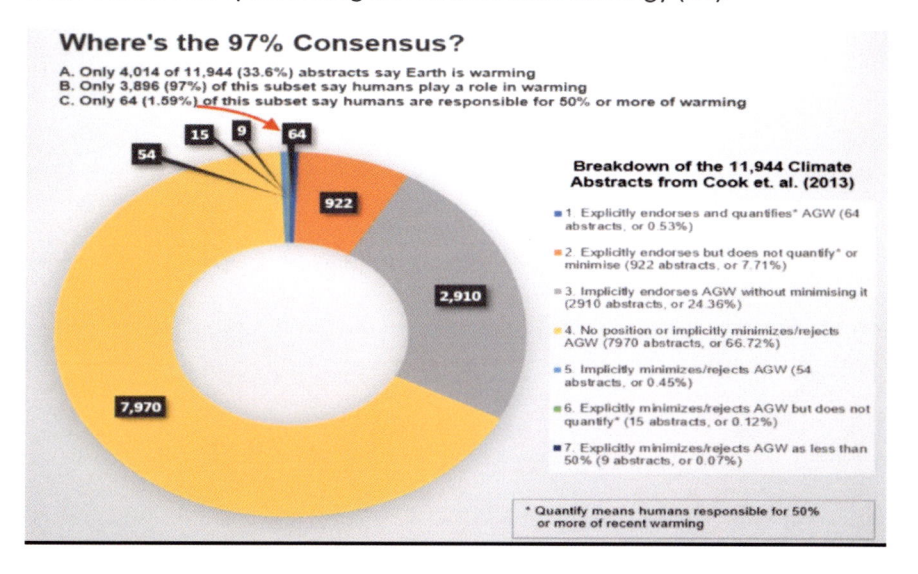

**Where's the 97% Consensus?**

A. Only 4,014 of 11,944 (33.6%) abstracts say Earth is warming
B. Only 3,896 (97%) of this subset say humans play a role in warming
C. Only 64 (1.59%) of this subset say humans are responsible for 50% or more of warming

**Breakdown of the 11,944 Climate Abstracts from Cook et. al. (2013)**

- 1. Explicitly endorses and quantifies* AGW (64 abstracts, or 0.53%)
- 2. Explicitly endorses but does not quantify* or minimise (922 abstracts, or 7.71%)
- 3. Implicitly endorses AGW without minimising it (2910 abstracts, or 24.36%)
- 4. No position or implicitly minimizes/rejects AGW (7970 abstracts, or 66.72%)
- 5. Implicitly minimizes/rejects AGW (54 abstracts, or 0.45%)
- 6. Explicitly minimizes/rejects AGW but does not quantify* (15 abstracts, or 0.12%)
- 7. Explicitly minimizes/rejects AGW as less than 50% (9 abstracts, or 0.07%)

* Quantify means humans responsible for 50% or more of recent warming

The most notable promoter of the climate crisis is Greta Thunberg a teenage school dropout and a corrupt Politian called Al Gore. Greta gets a huge amount of air time in the media yet is just an activist, her climate knowledge and understanding is the epitome of junk science. Al Gore who made and promoted a film called an inconvenient truth which stated the ice caps would be gone by 2013, they're still there. In fact every prediction in his film was wildly off the mark. The film was also banned for use in UK schools as it was an obvious propaganda piece that scared the wits out of the impressionable minds of children.

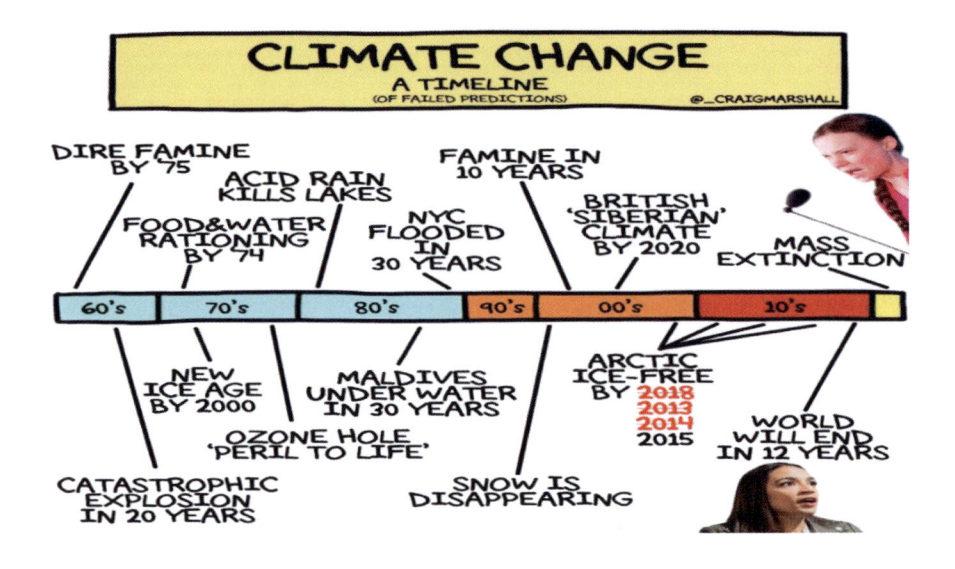

## CLIMATE CHANGE
### A TIMELINE
(OF FAILED PREDICTIONS)

@_CRAIGMARSHALL

- DIRE FAMINE BY '75
- ACID RAIN KILLS LAKES
- FOOD & WATER RATIONING BY '74
- FAMINE IN 10 YEARS
- NYC FLOODED IN 30 YEARS
- BRITISH 'SIBERIAN' CLIMATE BY 2020
- MASS EXTINCTION

60's | 70's | 80's | 90's | 00's | 10's

- NEW ICE AGE BY 2000
- MALDIVES UNDER WATER IN 30 YEARS
- ARCTIC ICE-FREE BY 2018 2013 2014 2015
- WORLD WILL END IN 12 YEARS
- OZONE HOLE 'PERIL TO LIFE'
- CATASTROPHIC EXPLOSION IN 20 YEARS
- SNOW IS DISAPPEARING

Unfortunately the left prefer indoctrination over education as long as it aligns with their radical activis or ideology. It should be noted these so called climate activists fly everywhere via private jet, have huge houses that gives them a carbon footprint larger than your average town. Incidentally the carbon footprint line was actually a marketing campaign utilised by BP to green wash and guilt trip individuals into thinking excess CO2 is their fault and not the fault of oil giants (33).

The biggest fraud of the lefts climate change ideology can still be viewed even with the current level of censorship. These two documents are I believe the smoking gun of the climate scam. First we have the climate gate emails which highlighted leading climate scientists in the UK and the US colluding to change the temperature data as it didn't fit their pre conceived warming data (34). They also tried to hide the fact that temperature hasn't followed $CO_2$ levels throughout history, in modern times $CO_2$ didn't follow the temperature for over 800 years.

## CO₂ lags behind temperatures

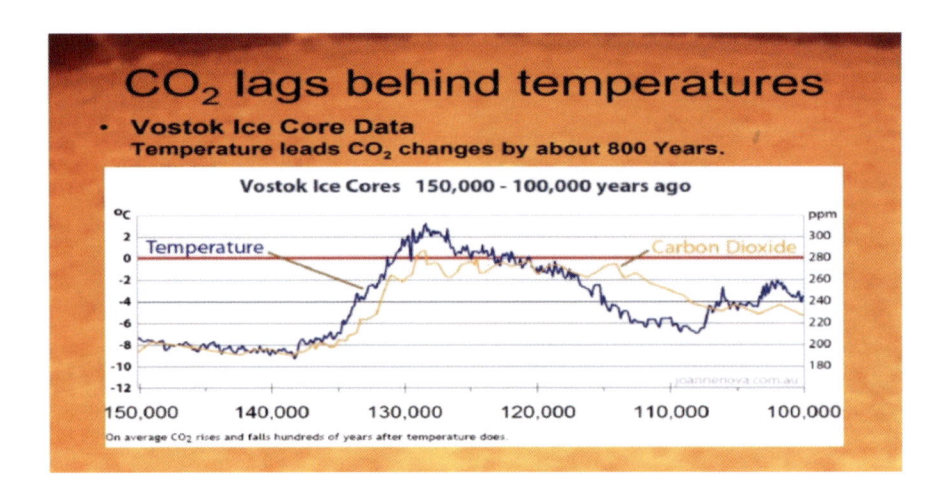

- **Vostok Ice Core Data**
  Temperature leads CO₂ changes by about 800 Years.

*Vostok Ice Cores 150,000 - 100,000 years ago*

(Chart showing Temperature and Carbon Dioxide curves from 150,000 to 100,000 years ago, with temperature in °C ranging from -12 to 2, and CO₂ in ppm ranging from 180 to 300.)

On average CO₂ rises and falls hundreds of years after temperature does.

Secondly we can still view the original 1990 climate change data on the IPCC website, they've made it incredibly hard to find but with a bit of time and effort it's still there. What it highlights is that the Mann et al. Hockey stick graph (which most of the ideology is based) is completely manipulated and skewed with fake data. Looking at the 1990 document the medieval warm period and little ice age are still intact and the temperature continues to rise and fall like it always has, it certainly doesn't go up continually like the hockey stick graph! (35).

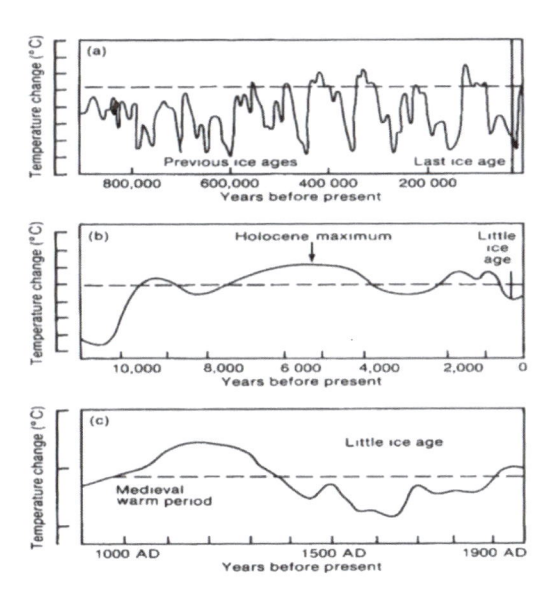

**Figure 7.1:** Schematic diagrams of global temperature variations since the Pleistocene on three time scales (a) the last million years (b) the last ten thousand years and (c) the last thousand years. The dotted line nominally represents conditions near the beginning of the twentieth century.

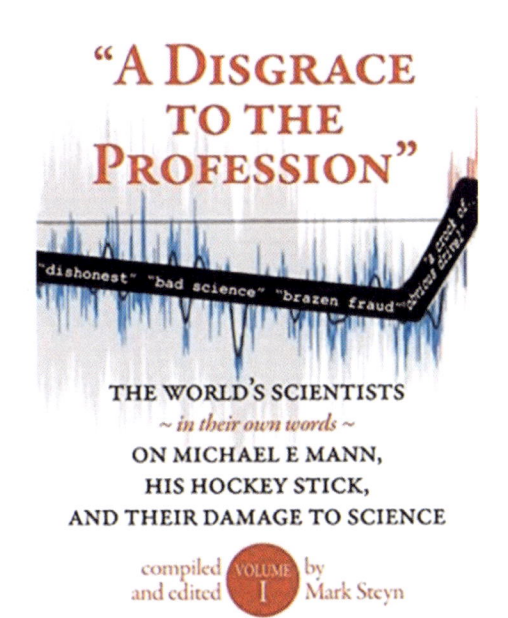

# "A DISGRACE TO THE PROFESSION"

"dishonest" "bad science" "brazen fraud"

### THE WORLD'S SCIENTISTS
~ *in their own words* ~
ON MICHAEL E MANN,
HIS HOCKEY STICK,
AND THEIR DAMAGE TO SCIENCE

compiled and edited VOLUME I by Mark Steyn

Manipulation of weather data is nothing new, remember when the entire spotlight was on the ozone layer and the use of CFC gases? Well it seems that was another attempt at invisible threats of doom. The narrative was that the ozone layer was opening year after year over Antarctica and there was also a hole opening above the US. The Montreal Protocol was developed which banned companies from making their products containing certain CFC's, the protocol was hailed a major success and governing bodies made considerable profits from fining said companies use of CFC gases. However, one look at the data and you can clearly see that there never was a hole opening over the US and that the ozone layer hole over Antarctica hasn't changed in size despite the banning of all CFC gases (36). Much like the global temperature you could easily conclude that it is merely getting smaller and bigger on a natural cycle.

There never was a Northern Hemisphere Ozone Hole, and the one over Antarctica has not changed in size since the CFC ban was implemented.

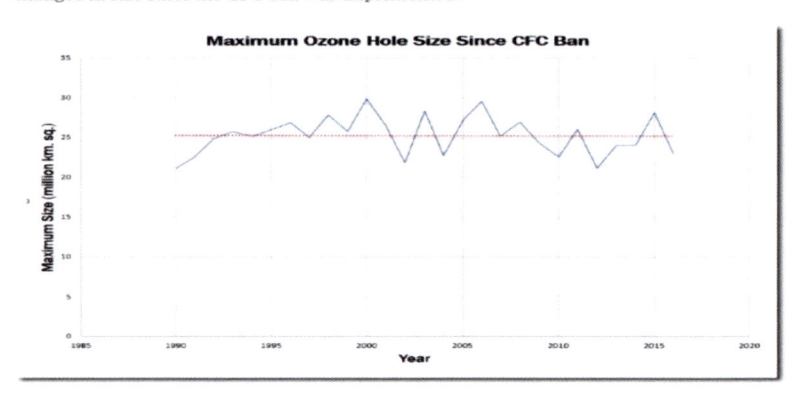

**Maximum Ozone Hole Size Since CFC Ban**

https://ozonewatch.gsfc.nasa.gov/statistics/ytd_data.txt

The whole woke movement has been best described by one of the best minds of a generation, Thomas Sowell, see below... Especially the climate crisis ideology which if accepted and implemented will have catastrophic effects on society. We're already seeing the issues with banning/limiting fossil fuels without having a readymade alternative and it's only going to get worse!

> Activism is a way for useless people to feel important, even if the consequences of their activism are counterproductive for those they claim to be helping and damaging to the fabric of society as a whole.
>
> — *Thomas Sowell*

The radical left would do well to realise that they are dabbling with radical ideology. Radical ideology aligned with communist/socialist tendencies has a 100% failure rate throughout history. The last westernised population to dabble in radical ideology was Hitler and the Nazi's, the left should note that Nazi ideology was accepted by the general population as appropriate and promoted by the academics of the time much like with the woke ideology of today. In the book 'The Fourth Turning' they point to the fact that populations lose their minds and morals every 80-100 years, the reason being that people who live a relatively easy life have the time to dwell on ideology and become weak people whereas populations who had previously lead hard lives became strong individuals and didn't have time to dabble or even think about radical ideology when survival was their main goal of the day. Another factor I believe is the elimination of religion in the youth of today, I'm not a religious man but I do believe in a creator. Faith in previous generations had kept people in check and enabled them to have strong family morals and values. These days without faith youngsters are left to find their values on social media and being that they have impressionable minds they fall deep into harmful indoctrination and ideology. Even in schools they have replaced hymns and prayer, which was a daily occurrence in my day, and replaced it with gender ideology and other radical ideologies.

| Saeculum | Time from climax of Crisis to climax of Awakening | (climax year) Awakening (full era) | Time from climax of Awakening to climax of Crisis | (climax year) Crisis (full era) | Time from one Crisis climax to next Crisis climax |
|---|---|---|---|---|---|
| LATE MEDIEVAL | | | | (1485) Wars of the Roses (1459–1487) | |
| REFORMATION | 51 years | (1536) Protestant Reformation (1517–1542) | 52 years | (1588) Armada Crisis (1569–1594) | 103 years |
| NEW WORLD | 52 years | (1640) Puritan Awakening (1621–1649) | 49 years | (1689) Glorious Revolution (1675–1704) | 101 years |
| REVOLUTIONARY | 52 years | (1741) Great Awakening (1727–1746) | 40 years | (1781) American Revolution (1773–1794) | 92 years |
| CIVIL WAR | 50 years | (1831) Transcendental Awakening (1822–1844) | 32 years | (1863) Civil War (1860–1865) | 82 years |
| GREAT POWER | 33 years | (1896) Third Great Awakening (1886–1908) | 48 years | (1944) Great Depression and World War II (1929–1946) | 81 years |
| MILLENNIAL | 30 years | (1974) Consciousness Revolution (1964–1984) | 51 years? | (2025?) Millennial Crisis? (2005?–2026?) | 81 years |

HARD TIMES CREATE STRONG MEN

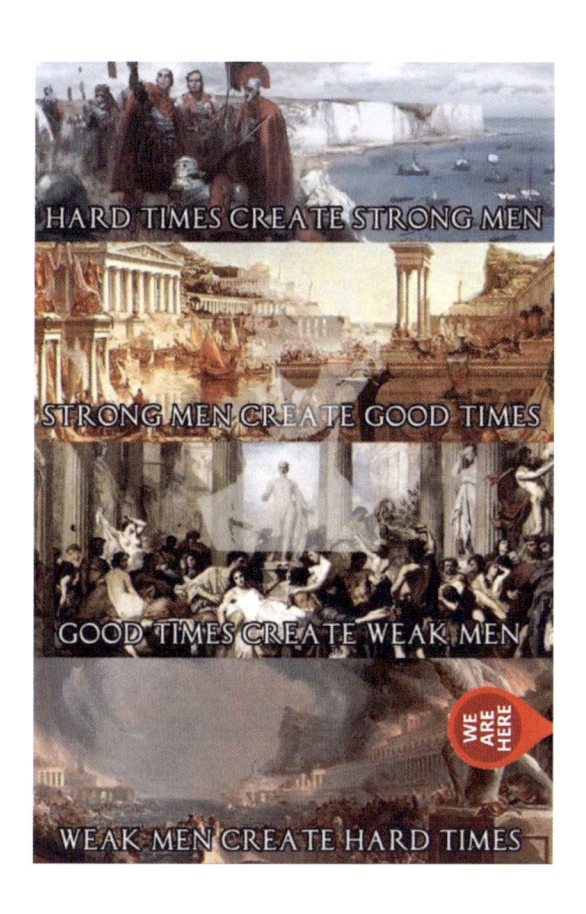

STRONG MEN CREATE GOOD TIMES

GOOD TIMES CREATE WEAK MEN

WE ARE HERE

WEAK MEN CREATE HARD TIMES

# Chapter 5 - Scams & More Scams

Having read 217 books from December 2022 to December 2023 it has come to my attention that most government institutions and government policy is designed to impoverish the population and line the pockets of the elite. If you really understand how things work its literally scam after scam coupled with a bit of distraction. From the scientific process, pharmaceutical industry, energy companies, politics, the media, wars and the banking system, it's all designed to scare you into submission and take your hard earned cash, but never question it or you're labelled a quack or god forbid a conspiracy theorist!? It's high time we strip back all these sectors and start a fresh with a democratically voted system for each.

The scientific process in today's format is a million miles away from the process of years gone by. Unfortunately it has been hijacked by wealthy elites looking to push their agendas. Most scientific process nowadays is model based; the problem here is that any preconceived views or results can be implemented before the study begins. Therefore you get the results you're looking for rather than the reality of the results; you also get rewarded by your wealthy elitist donor who is more than happy with the skewed results that favour his agenda. Look no further than the covid lockdown and vaccine science as a good example. Neil Ferguson of SAGE used his computer model which told us lockdown was the only way to save millions of lives, this prediction was wildly wrong as per all of his past predictions on bird flu and mad cow disease which were also all wildly off the mark, but they still continue to use his model? why? Because it enabled the wealthy elites and billionaires to make billions of dollars while small businesses were decimated, the biggest wealth transfer in human history, it's estimated 3 trillion dollars were taken from the general population and added to the fortunes of billionaires. Lockdowns were later shown to have killed far more people than they saved by way of suicide and missed medical appointments. Nowadays we have the alliance effect where everyone has preconceived ideological theories and that's exactly what they look for and find. Hard non-political science is now unfortunately a thing of the past, what we're left with is agenda bias pseudoscience marketed as hard science. If any proper hard science comes to light the media always censor or ignore it so the unwitting general public, BBC news watchers only know one narrative, truly Orwellian!

The covid vaccine was much of the same, it was only mentioned positively in the media and any dissenters were censored or labelled an anti-vaxxer or covid denier, whatever that means? They are used in the same context as conspiracy theorist or climate denier, they make no sense yet the normie public would rather spout out anti-vaxxer or conspiracy theorist rather than do any independent research, they more like weaponised language to prevent the critique of the power structure to me. By the way the term conspiracy theorist was developed by the CIA in the 1960's as a way to stop people questioning the Kennedy assassination, this isn't a conspiracy, and the document is now declassified and viewable. As you can see below…

CLASSIFIED MESSAGE
SECRET

CMO: RICHARD HELMS
UNIT: DDP
EXT: 5353
DATE: 30 APRIL 64

TO: LONDON
FROM: DIRECTOR
CONF: DDP
INFO: *DCI, D/DCI, C/CI, C/CI/SI, C/WH, VR

TO: LOND
FOR FELS

CITE DIR 16228

PLEASE AIR MAIL PROMPTLY TO MR. ALLEN DULLES, 2723 Q STREET, WASHINGTON, ADVANCE COPY OR REGULAR COPY SOON AS AVAILABLE OF BOOK BY THOMAS BUCHANAN RE WHO ALLEGEDLY RESPONSIBLE FOR DEATH PRESIDENT KENNEDY. UNDERSTAND BOOK BEING PUBLISHED IN LONDON BY SECKER AND WARBURG. STATION SHOULD ABSORB CHARGES.

END OF MESSAGE

CS COMMENT: * DISSEMINATION APPLICABLE TO GPFLOOR CABLES.

EYES ONLY
2

On 18 June 1962, DCI McCone and Helms briefed Secretary of State Rusk generally on the operation without going into operational details. Later on the same day, President John F. Kennedy was briefed. _____ occurred somewhat later, and on 15 April 1963, DCI McCone met with President Kennedy alone and briefed the President on the details of this new phase of the operation. On the same day, the Attorney General was briefed and he agreed that he would not mention it to the FBI unless the FBI themselves raised it with him. On 3 February 1964, DCI McCone met alone with President Lyndon B. Johnson and briefed him on the operation. On 4 February McGeorge Bundy was briefed. On 6 February 1964 in a briefing of Secretary of State Rusk on the results of the operation, Rusk expressed reservations about the propriety of such an operation. He raised this same concern in subsequent conversations with McCone on 17 April 1964, 28 May 1964, and 14 June 1964. On 12 September 1964 Rusk continued to express grave reservations and repeatedly suggested that _____

_____ In a meeting on 28 May 1964 Rusk expressed these reservations in the presence of DCI McCone and President John F. Kennedy. Secretary of Defense McNamara was also present, and there is no record that he had previously been made aware of this operation.

4. Although certain activities never got beyond the planning stage, there are, I believe, three examples of such planning which could be subject to misinterpretation. One involved chemical warfare operations. _____ A second involved a paramilitary strike against _____ _____ Outside the United States Government, General Eisenhower was briefed on such planning. A third, which assumes a new significance today, involved a proposal by Angleton and Helms for a greatly increased intelligence collection effort against foreign installations in this country. This planning also involved a scheme for selected

SECRET/SENSITIVE
EYES ONLY

00458

Like the lockdowns the vaccine was labelled our saviour of the pandemic, the problem was the vaccine didn't work, wasn't tested enough and has since been removed from general use over safety concerns. To me it was pretty obvious from day one that it was mostly propaganda to sell vaccines, I mean what other medication can you give to the population of the earth multiple times? its a drug pushers wet dream! The first piece of propaganda I spotted was they weren't even sure if a vaccine was possible, then out of nowhere 4/5 companies all found the answer at the same time. Next they stated the vaccine was safe and effective as it was released to the general public, how did they know with no long term data? more provable propaganda, and all governments were pushing the same line in lockstep stating that the vaccine was safe and stopped transmission (V20). Next we had the take the vaccine to save granny line, then when they realised it didn't stop transmission they updated their propaganda to the vaccines prevent deaths and hospitalisation, again provable propaganda as there have been no randomised controlled studies on severity of symptoms between the vaxxed vs unvaxxed. In fact the scientific process has become so unreliable and misleading I'd say its no more dependable than politics as highlighted in this study (37) that found that 90% of peer reviewed studies can't be repeated, even the peer reviewed system is corrupt. Firstly if your study or findings are not in line with the current narrative then your study will be rejected for peer review, what your left with is an echo chamber of people who agree, no matter if their right or wrong. This is the opposite of the actual scientific process which should be to hypothesise for further research, not to end debate and label something settled science as you hear so much today, that's the opposite of scientific process.

The pharmaceutical industry is much the same, nowadays the big pharma companies lobby the politicians and governments and give them untold fortunes to promote and sell their products. This was highlighted brilliantly during the pandemic with all western G7 governments using the same propaganda in lockstep to push the vaccines for the drug companies regardless of safety and efficacy. The pharmaceutical scientific process is also set up for the company's profit margins not the wellbeing of the population. For starters most medication is merely to mask symptoms, they won't cure you but they will keep you coming back for more, stay away from medicine, use it as a last resort only. Then you have conventional doctors who dismiss any alternate medicine or treatment for the reason that it has had no human clinical trials. Here lies the problem, any natural or holistic treatment can't be patented because you can't patent natural remedies and re-purposed or holistic drugs have usually had their patent end years ago, simply put, the pharmaceutical companies and governing bodies won't spend the £100,000,000+ on the clinical trials if they can't patent the drug and make obscene amounts of money off the back of the drugs even if the holistic treatment has had incredible results in animal and independent human trials. It's a sad world we live in where profit is put before health and wellbeing.

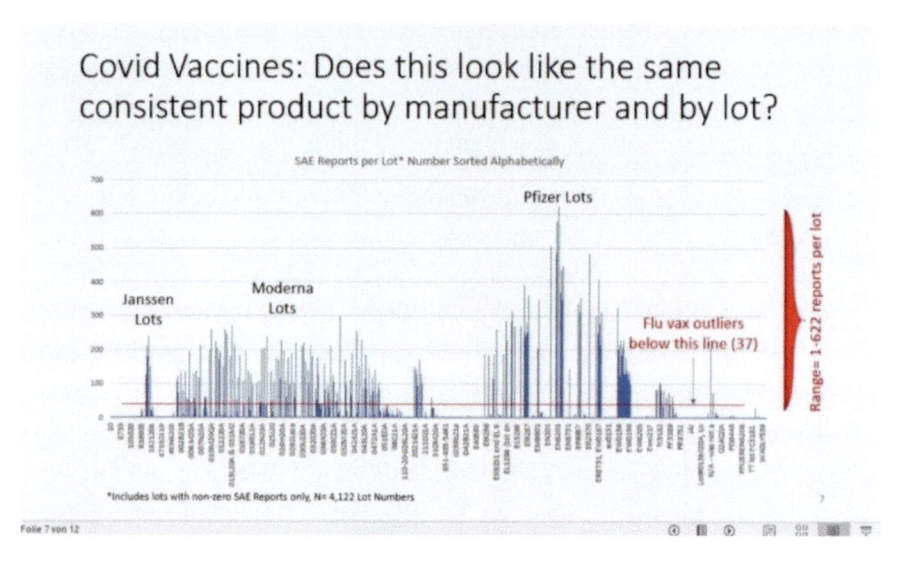

## Covid Vaccines: Does this look like the same consistent product by manufacturer and by lot?

*SAE Reports per Lot* Number Sorted Alphabetically*

Janssen Lots — Moderna Lots — Pfizer Lots — Flu vax outliers below this line (37)

Range= 1-622 reports per lot

*Includes lots with non-zero SAE Reports only, N= 4,122 Lot Numbers

Politics today is to placate the population into thinking they have a choice, nothing else. The people never get what they want, special interests always get their way via lobbying politicians. Its no wonder politicians have a £200-£300k salary per year yet usually leave parliament with a fortune of untold millions. Take a look at the US politicians view on the vaccine when Trump was still president (V21). Just look at war mongering former presidents and prime ministers, Blair, Bush and Obama to name a few who now seem to be worth hundreds of millions, due to their compliance with the military industrial complex no doubt, they always seem to fall into cushy jobs, Like Blair who is funded by the World Economic Forum and still gets plenty of media air time pushing the WEF digital ID and vaccine passport agenda, even though he should most probably be in jail. But in the backwards clown world we live in the person who published Blair and Bushes war crimes is the one locked up, Julian Assange is looking at a 175 year sentence for outing the crimes while the ones who knowingly committed the crimes are wealthy beyond belief and living a life of luxury. Remember back to the Iraq war which was based solely on false pretences of weapons of mass destruction? and the 45 minute to attack? Propaganda to enable public support is not new, you probably just didn't recognise it. Nowadays most politicians are owned by corporate interests, this is most prominent in the G7 politicians who are mostly members of the World Economic Forum and obviously paid to push the WEF's agenda. This would explain all G7 nations making the same mistakes in lockstep during the pandemic, they were following WEF guidelines not their own. Basically, if you identify with a single political party you've already lost, similarly, if all your beliefs align with a single political party then they're not your ideas, you're part of a tribalistic cult and most probably under mind control. All parties have good and bad ideas and policies, it's best to align yourself with all the ideas you agree with at either end of the political compass, negating good ideas simply because it's not the party you align with is a good sign that you're under mind control.

The media in today's form is now the opposite of what it used to be. Journalism in the mainstream is as good as dead, now were just left with a handful of actual independent journalists who get zero mainstream air time. Mainstream media is all owned by the same people, all companies report on the same issues and all blank out what doesn't align with their owner's narrative. This was highlighted during the pandemic where any descent regarding vaccines or lockdown was not even reported on, so much for balanced debate! There were multiple marches against lockdowns, vaccine coercion and government policy in London and also around the world yet they went unnoticed by the BBC or other major news channels. The BBC runs the worlds news alliance which is the head propaganda tool worldwide (V22), what you get is the exact same stories being distributed by all major news channels worldwide and also ignoring the exact same stories which don't align with the narrative, very dystopian! right out of 1984. Fortunately we have social media such as Twitter which still enables the average Joe to make informed decisions regarding world events, if you don't think something on the news sits right, you can go onto Twitter and people are posting live footage so you can get sense of what's true and what's not. I believe his is the reason they are trying to censor the internet and social media, they only want one source of truth, their propaganda! In true Orwellian fashion we also now have the thought police, I mean fact checkers. Now these fact checkers were never a thing before people knew the truth and could verify themselves via the internet. These fact checkers are merely a propaganda arm of the media, owned by the same people. One man who has his tentacles in everything is Bill Gates, supposedly a philanthropist, I'd say more a charlatan, he not only holds major stakes and influence in the vaccine companies but he also has huge stakes in major media companies, oh and you guessed it, he funds the fact checking organisations who lie through their teeth to hide Bills dodgy dealings with Jeffery Epstein and the likes (24).

The American war machine has been a prominent force since the 2nd World War, all of their invasions comes with some level of controversy. The same elites are known to fund both sides of all US wars; in fact they provided weapons for both sides in the 2nd World War. Nowadays the industrial military complex is the major player in weapons and lobby congress to buy and distribute their weapons. War is merely an elitist tool to take money from tax payers while pillaging nations of valuable resources. Given that there have been numerous wars throughout history what you need to remember is they know exactly what causes wars, they know exactly what prevents wars and they know how much money can be made from a war. Along with each war has come huge media propaganda campaigns to push for public support to invade, quite simply without the propaganda nobody would favour war, what the media does is make the so called enemy seem like a non-human satanic threat, that way the public lose the ability to think critically and go along with the propaganda. A small look into each invasion it becomes clear each war either starts with a false flag event (see gulf of Tonkin, Vietnam) or a huge propaganda push in the media. The invasion of Iraq was based on the propaganda of weapons of mass destruction, whereas anyone with any critical thought ability can see it was to steal Iraq oil. Afghanistan, you had the Muslim extremist and terrorist propaganda, I fell for that one, I remember being petrified being on a plane with a Muslim wearing a turban. The Afghan war was actually because the US wanted the lithium which is in abundance in Afghanistan. Then there is the opium fields which the US soldiers took over, you can only guess why they wanted the opium! Not forgetting the US actually established the Taliban during the cold war and called them freedom fighters, they even fought alongside them during the cold war, see Rambo. Now we have the invasion of Ukraine, although the US have not fought in the war they have provided billions of dollars' worth of weapons to the Ukrainian soldiers. Again a mass propaganda push against Russia and for Ukraine has been pushed in the mainstream media, the same Ukraine which was previously vilified as being very right wing and having Azoz Nazi battalions, now apparently they're freedom fighters. Then you get all the sheep putting Ukraine flags up everywhere without knowing the ins and outs, they just follow the crowd and believe the media unquestionably.

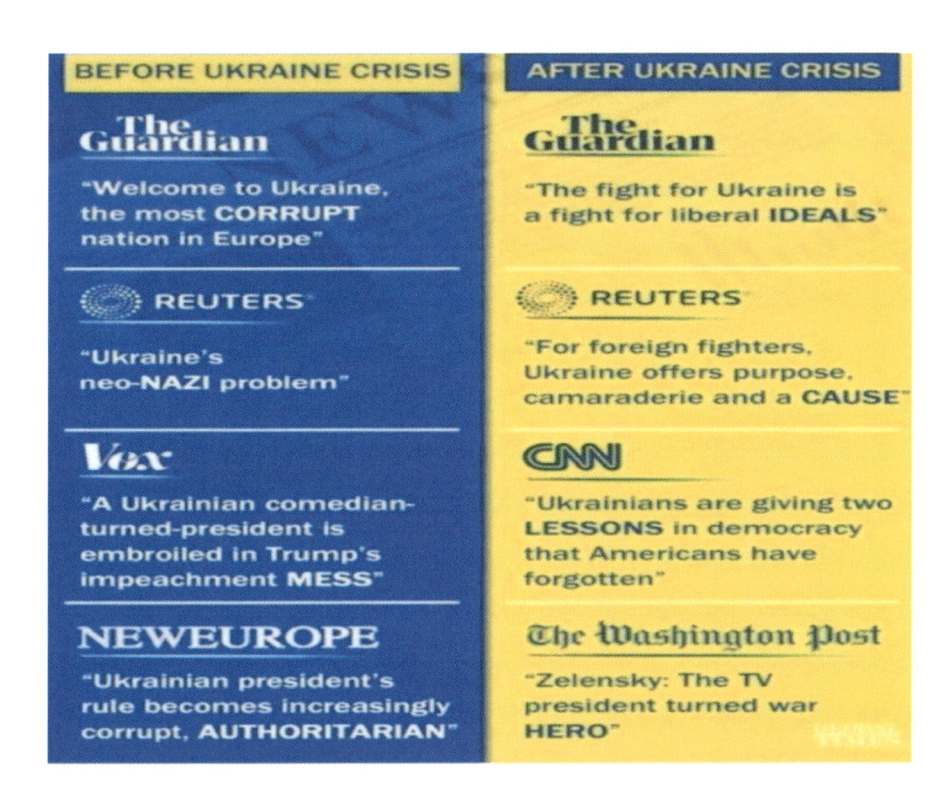

| BEFORE UKRAINE CRISIS | AFTER UKRAINE CRISIS |
|---|---|
| **The Guardian** — "Welcome to Ukraine, the most **CORRUPT** nation in Europe" | **The Guardian** — "The fight for Ukraine is a fight for liberal **IDEALS**" |
| **REUTERS** — "Ukraine's neo-**NAZI** problem" | **REUTERS** — "For foreign fighters, Ukraine offers purpose, camaraderie and a **CAUSE**" |
| **Vox** — "A Ukrainian comedian-turned-president is embroiled in Trump's impeachment **MESS**" | **CNN** — "Ukrainians are giving two **LESSONS** in democracy that Americans have forgotten" |
| **NEWEUROPE** — "Ukrainian president's rule becomes increasingly corrupt, **AUTHORITARIAN**" | **The Washington Post** — "Zelensky: The TV president turned war **HERO**" |

One listen to Putin and the Russian federation and their demands sound very reasonable. Since 2014 Russia asked that Ukraine remain neutral and don't join NATO. Instead Ukraine allowed NATO to establish rocket launchers on the Russian boarder, now imagine Canada or Mexico doing this on the US boarder? do you think there'd be any retaliation? But in the media Putin is Hitler and little Nazi Zelensky is a hero doing all his green screen media reports, meeting with celebs and politicians and no doubt filtering all that US cash through for his elite masters, I wonder how Zelensky is a billionaire? Now Ukraine are the in nation with the left they seem to forget that Ukraine are mostly right wing Nazi's and they also seem to forget all the other nations who are under constant attack by the US, another clear hypocrisy. Julian Assange states that all war has a purpose and that purpose is and I quote "The goal is to use war to wash money out of the tax bases of the US & Europe through Afghanistan and back into the hands of a transnational security elite. The goal is an endless war, not a successful war" Why do they hate Putin so much? (V24a)

Maybe because he's not compliant with the G7 western build back better agenda. The sanctions put on Russia have worked in their favour, they now have a partnership with China to sell oil and gas and their currency is one if the strongest of the last couple of years, the sanctions have only been detrimental to Europe, it's almost like we've sanctioned ourselves. By the way no previous sanctions in history have had any impact, which makes you think the sanctions are nefarious and actually aimed and bringing down the EU countries all ready for a great reset.

## US/UK/EU SANCTIONS

| COUNTRY | DATE SANCTIONS IMPOSED | OBJECTIVE OF SANCTIONS | SUCCESS OR FAIL |
|---|---|---|---|
| Cuba | 1962 | Regime change | ✖ |
| Iran | 1979 | Regime change | ✖ |
| Venezuela | 2005 | Regime change | ✖ |
| Syria | 2011 | Regime change | ✖ |

Russia and China are the only nations strong enough to stand up to the western elites that's why they're demonised, basically any nation that is a threat to western one world domination will be vilified, the only reason the US haven't gone after these nations themselves is that they don't go after nations with nukes, it's too risky and the US army is now so weakened by woke ideology that they're more concerned with pronouns than combat.

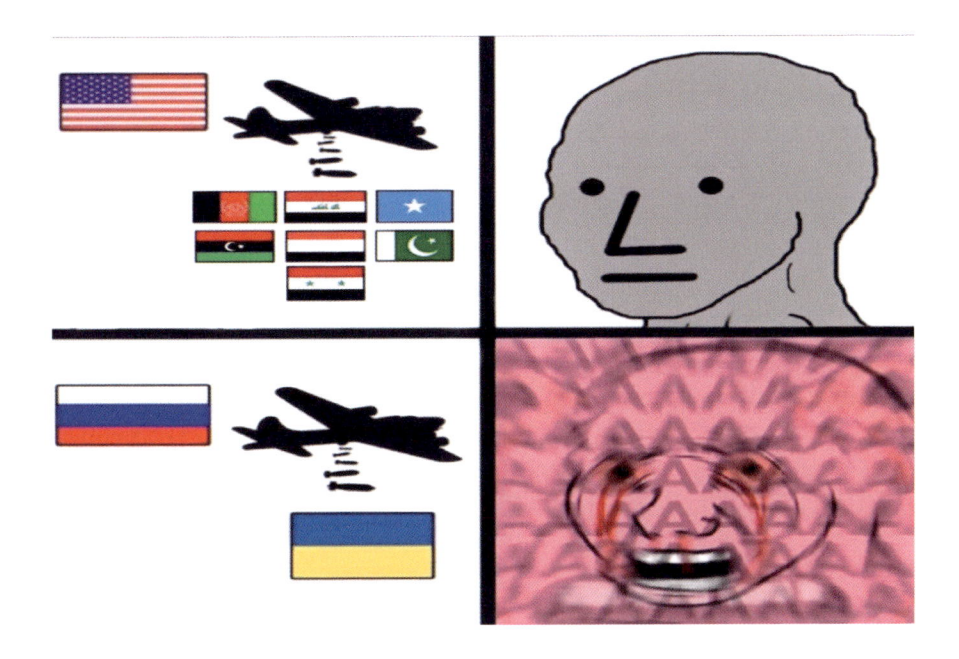

The biggest scam known to man is the current monetary banking system. If every man knew how the banking system actually worked I'm sure there'd be a revolution within days. This is how it works, fractional reserve banking, which means the banks get to lend out unlimited amounts of money (money they don't have) and lend it to you at a high interest, so they're making money from you by lending you money they don't have. All central banks have the ability to print money at will, it's all digits on a screen, 97% of money is digital only 3% is physical cash. The UK came off the gold backed standard in 1914 and the US under Nixon in 1971. Now the money is not backed by anything it can be printed in unlimited amounts, the problem for the average Joe is that it debases their money, for instance if you had £1000 in your account and then the central bank had 1 trillion pounds then printed another trillion pounds then your £1000 is now worth a measly £500. It's basically legal counterfeit, if you or I tried to print some cash we'd be in jail in no time. The extra cash in the system then has a knock on effect on society in the form of inflation. The media will tell you that inflation is transitory or corporate greed but it's just an alibi for government negligence. The only true cause of inflation in money printing, listen to any top tier economist and they'll tell you the same thing, see Friedman or Sowell (V23). Over the last two decades the US have printed more cash than they did in the last 200 years, what could go wrong? I think things are going to get bad very soon. To note, the Federal Reserve is the central bank of the US but is not federal and has no reserves. It is an independent company with no money yet gets to print and distribute unlimited cash to banks; the same can be said for UK and EU banks which are governed by the BICS central bank in Switzerland. You may wonder why you pay so much tax given that the powers above can simply print money at will; surely they don't need our cash? How can they steal 40% of our income yet still find themselves in 30 trillion of debt? It can't be negligence, it seems more like a controlled demolition, they know what causes inflation and they still proceed to print more cash, almost like they're setting up a huge crash to then offer everyone they're saviour of a central bank digital currency slave system. It should also be noted that income tax did not exist until 1913 the same year the Federal Reserve was established, shock! Governments don't produce anything worthwhile, all their policies are dependent on our cash, we're paying for our own demise.

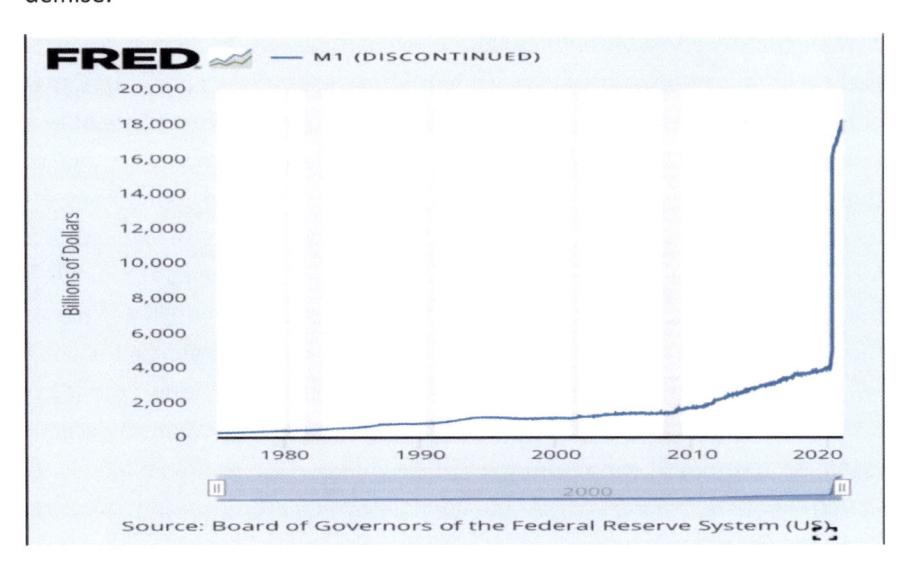

What can we do about these scams? First off we need to pinpoint the most important scams to the elites. I believe the elites have controlled us via media and money predominantly, their two main tools. Without the media they can't feed us their propaganda and fake news and without cash they can't control and micro manage our every life move. We already have the answer to the media, the internet... this is the reason the governments of the world are hell bent on censoring certain people and certain narratives. They simply want to be the only source of information weather it's the truth or not. With a decentralised internet the population has the freedom to follow independent journalists and to make their own informed choice on narratives, this is why its imperative that we keep the internet uncensored and enable free speech for everyone, you may not agree with what they say but you should know they have every right to say it. There are currently protocols being developed to keep the internet decentralised, decentralised simply means it's not centrally controlled i.e. it is simply governed by the people who make all the decisions via governance vote. Nowadays we have Twetch which runs on Bitcoin SV that is a decentralised Twitter, we have Substack a decentralised journalist hub where you pay the journalist directly for their content. We have entire decentralised protocols being built to enable a new decentralised internet like Tomi Net which is building a decentralised internet from scratch.

This brings me onto money, the G7 governments and beyond are currently implementing a CBDC (central bank digital currency) which is basically a cryptocurrency but a centralised version. Being centralised this means the money can be programmed to have time limits so you have to spend it by a certain date, it can be programmed to only be used for certain items and can be programmed to be rejected if the government deem you nefarious or even if you have the wrong political views. This CBDC fits nicely with a social credit system which is already in place along with vaccine passports in China, you may have noticed no world government hs condemned the China social credit system or the China approach to covid, why? Because that's exactly what they want to do! The only way to stand against this tyranny is mass noncompliance, don't use their media platforms, don't use their money. But what else is there? To start with we have Bitcoin BTC. BTC is the original crypto currency dating back to 2009, once thought to be a scam it is now traded in the billions of dollars a day and incidentally is the number one investment of the last 20 years by factors of thousands. Most people think of BTC as a currency however, it's not great as a currency, its slow to process transactions, it does not scale and is expensive to use especially if dealing with small transaction amounts. What people fail to realise is the technology BTC is built on, blockchain. Blockchain is an un-censorable, immovable and transparent protocol where any data can be stored forever and is not able to be deleted, imagine if we had that since day one! It's a protocol that can potentially take on Silicon Valley as a single protocol, you can have the internet, banking transactions, all word data, science, books everything in one protocol, it's easily the single biggest invention of the 21st century and what's stranger its creator is an unknown anonymous coder. He went by the synonym Satoshi Nakamoto while creating BTC and confirming on the Bitcoin chat forum, then disappeared never to be heard of again in 2010. The problem with BTC is that is doesn't scale so can't really be used efficiently as a currency. There was a blockchian war circa 2017 where the BTC core developers had disagreements on the direction of BTC. This made way for Bitcoin to split into 3 separate versions each taking BTC core developers with them. First we have BTC or core Bitcoin, which is the current market leader but favours small blocks. Then we have BCH Bitcoin cash which as the name would suggest has larger blocks and can scale to meet the demands of a mass currency. Lastly there is Bitcoin BSV or Bitcoin Satoshi Vision, this version kept the original ethos of Sataoshi Nakamoto which was to use Bitcoin as a p2p cash system that can scale huge amounts of transactions at any one time, even miniscule ones at a fraction of the price. BSV has the potential to replace Silicon Valley as one single standalone protocol, this is the reason it's the most delisted, demonised crypto in the world, see a link here? It's constantly referred to as a scam and your average crypto noob thinks its trash, if they'd look into it I believe they'd see BSV as one of our greatest hopes against tyranny and corruption. It's also worth noting that quite impressively BSV, despite having a small market cap, already has over half of the entire crypto space in daily transactions.

## Market Capitalization, $USD

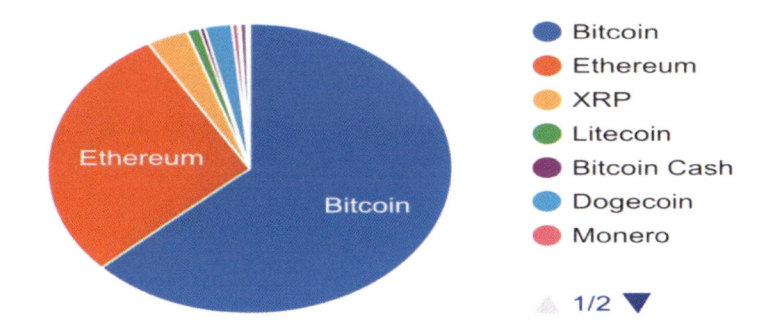

- Bitcoin
- Ethereum
- XRP
- Litecoin
- Bitcoin Cash
- Dogecoin
- Monero

1/2

## Transactions last 24h

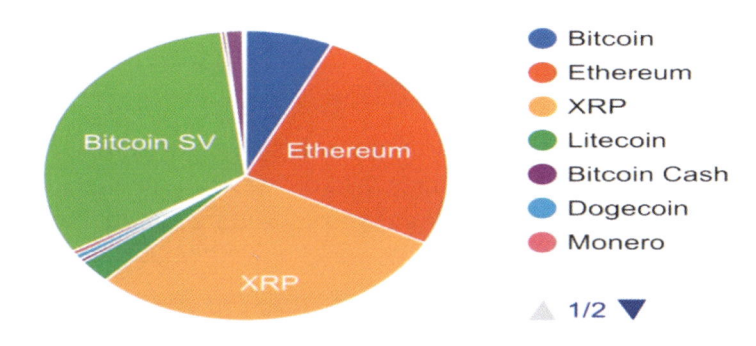

- Bitcoin
- Ethereum
- XRP
- Litecoin
- Bitcoin Cash
- Dogecoin
- Monero

1/2

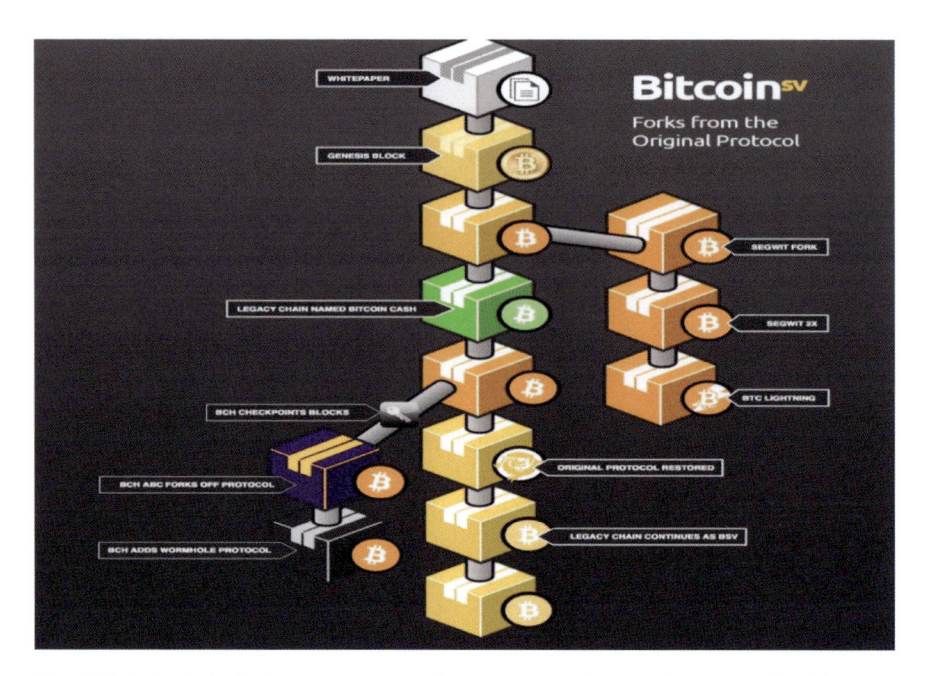

The BSV blockchain is transparent for a reason, it was developed with the idea to keep all transactions open to public view, imagine seeing exactly where all your tax money goes and what governments are really spending their money on!

On the other hand people should be able to have the option of privacy with their transactions like they do now with physical cash. Luckily there is a private cash protocol called Monero or better known as its ticker XMR. Unlike Bitcoin the Monero blockchain is completely private, it uses ring signatures to hide all transactions before finalising in your wallet without anyone knowing what you bought or how much you spent or have in your wallet, unlike Bitcoin which you can see every wallets amount and every transaction they've ever made. Again Monero is heavily demonised, the best line is that it's used by criminals, which it is, but like everything else also has more positives than negatives. The same narrative of only used by thieves was also used in the early days for BTC until it became compromised and is now I believe controlled by the elites and governments, that's why it's now promoted and not demonised. BTC was used on the dark net in the early days and now the favoured currency on the dark web is Monero, we'll have to wait and see if Monero eventually matches BTC in terms of price and adoption but it's certainly a decent bet in my opinion. What we need to remember is that this is the 4th attempt at the Keynesian monetary system, it has a failure rate of 100%, it is designed to impoverish the population subtly through inflation or legal counterfeit. All cryptocurreny is based on the Austrian school ethos of a capped supply which makes sound money free from manipulation or inflation.

Below highlights the ease of use of Monero (XMR) in comparison to Bitcoin (BTC).

## Bitcoin Privacy Spending Cycle
*by @NimzoBit*

**KYC sats** — Swan — Take custody of your coins!! Withdraw from exchanges! — on-chain → Top up channel Lightning Wallet (1) — LN-waves → Lightning Wallet (2)

**Non-KYC sats** → Whirlpool mixing service → Samourai wallet and/or Sparrow wallet

**Cold storage** ← **Bitrefill** Spending coins

---

## MONERO PRIVACY SPENDING CYCLE

**GET MONERO**
Bisq
Localmonero
kycnot.me

---->

**USE MONERO**
Send it, spend it, hold it, swap it...
Low fees and fast

---

The mainstream argument about crypto is that it's not backed by anything; the funny thing is that it is backed by mathematics, each transaction has to be mined by computer hash power and a mathematical equation has to be worked out to confirm the block (transaction). Cash, known as fiat, on the other hand is absolutely positively backed by nothing apart from decree or law to you and I. It's only worth something because the government say it is or demand it for their services. We also have Gold and Silver which are better as a store of value but they lack the ability to cross boarders, good luck taking £50,000 of gold out of a tyrannical nation's government without it being stolen! You also have stocks which the mainstream favour over crypto, you have to understand that stocks are just an extension of the banking system, sure you can make a few quid if you select the correct stock but its heavily dependent on bankers and very easily manipulated, you think people like Warren Buffet would bet on a stock without some definite inside info? I don't think so. For this reason I'd recommend putting a significant amount of cash in BTC, BSV, XMR and some in gold and silver. Be warned though that crypto currency is still fledgling as a commodity and still relatively hard to use in comparison to cash. I'd recommend studying it significantly and performing a few micro transactions to make sure you understand the process thoroughly, it's not like using a bank, you're your own bank, any mistake can't be reversed. I've been using crypto since 2016 and studied it before I attempted to use it, I've still not lost any crypto, although I did make the mistake of saving my wallet keys on my phone note pad which was compromised and I lost the contents of my wallet, only ever write your wallet seed phases on physical paper!

> "Welcome to 2030. I own nothing, have no privacy, and life has never been better."
> - Ida Auken, Member of Parliament, Denmark

> "Welcome to 2030. I own an unknown amount of Monero, have lots of privacy and life has never been better."
> - Monero-chan

If you feel you want to get into crypto or feel the need to make your transactions private this is a handy table of how to either make sure your current crypto is completely private or if your yet to buy any crypto it shows you how to keep your crypto completely private from day one, it's one of the best and most useful diagrams I've come across, see below...

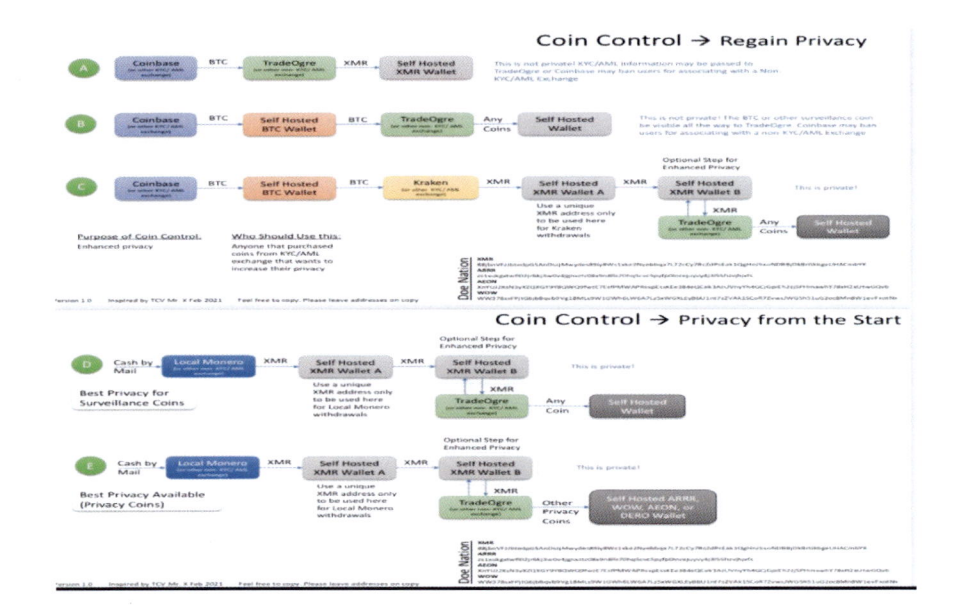

# Chapter 6 - What's Happening? Why? & What Can We Do?

At this point I can only hazard an informed educated guess regarding what exactly is going on through my own independent research. What seems feasible is that the governments of the G7 nations no longer working for their people. They now work for governing bodies such as the World Health Organisation WHO and the World Economic Forum WEF. The leader of the WEF Kluas Schwab is on record stating he has infiltrated most world governments; by the way this is no conspiracy. A conspiracy is defined as hidden nefarious planning, Klaus Schwab tells you what he's doing, read his book The Great Reset and it outlines his hopes and intensions for western society. He's clearly a communist and would like nothing more than to enslave humanity as he states "you will own nothing and be happy" he wants to end public ownership of everything. He wants you all driving electric cars, maybe because they can be remotely controlled and can be prevented from driving places the government deem unworthy. He wants to end gas and gas stoves, maybe because they can't be shut off remotely? He's a big promoter of the non-existent dangerous of covid and the climate crisis, maybe to scare you into compliance? Maybe he's pushing the climate crisis to enable a carbon tax system and enables the government to keep you confined to your town if you've gone over your carbon allowance, sounds much like the 15 minute cities being implemented and trailed in Oxfordshire, a carbon allowance that would by the way work perfectly in tandem with a social credit score and CBDC system, and then just like that we're all slaves and after a couple of generations our freedom will be gone forever and what's worse thanks to censorship nobody will remember how it used to be.

When I mention they or their I'm referring to elites and wealthy globalists, below is a rough idea of who the major players are who are working in lockstep with governments and devising this centralised planning for a one world governance, you'll never hear a bad word sais about this motley crew in the media. In no particular order...

- Klaus Scwab - Founder of The World Economic Forum
- Bill Gates - Bill & Melinda Gates Foundation
- Mark Zuckerberg - Facebook
- Henry Kissenger – Former US Security of State
- George Soros - The Open Foundation
- Ursula von der Leyen - President of the EU Commission
- Tedros Adhanom Ghebreyesus - Director of the World Health Organisation
- Vanguard & Blackrock

Then you have all the minion puppet politicians working in lockstep with these tyrants, most notably Joe Biden of the US, Justin Trudeu of Canada, Jacinda Arden of New Zealand, Dan Andrews in Australia, Macron of France and Rishi Sunak of the UK. Then you have the former politicians on the payroll also pushing the nefarious agenda, the likes of Tony Blair, Barak Obama, Hilary & Bill Clinton to name a few, all already should be in jail, we can only hope in the future! These elitist globalists use crisis as a tool, don't you think it's strange how many crisis have happened back to back? The pandemic or scamdemic as I call it (implementing an authoritarian regime), BLM destruction of cities (funded by the open society (George Soros)), the war in Ukraine (money laundering), the climate crisis hoax (more authoritarian policy change), the cost of living crisis, which by the way is caused by government policy, now they are trying to normalise it, like it's the general populations fault, etc. etc... These are all elitist tools to enable compliance through fear and to distract you from their nefarious central planning. These people know how to prevent all these crisis' as they've all happened before numerous times, the reason they don't prevent them is that they can use it to their advantage and they do exactly that, keep a look out for the next crisis! All of these crisis are obviously manufactured, these things don't happen all within a couple of years, the elites saw what ground they made with their agenda during the pandemic and want to keep the momentum going in their favour.

The worst of the lot is Trudeu of Canada, he states anyone who questions his policy as racist and right wing extremism. I'm not sure how right wing became a derogatory word, I'd say its much more acceptable to be right of centre than a far left extremist, what about far left extremism? There is far more of that about today and its very destructive to society. Trudeu then declared martial law on his own citizens after they sent a convoy of truckers to Ottawa outside of Canadian parliament to protest the vaccine mandates. Instead of spending time listening to his population he left Ottawa and hid in an unknown location while labelling the truckers and their supporters the fringe minority and sent armed militarised police into Ottawa to send the convoy packing. He also shut down the truckers bank accounts as well as anyone who donated to the truckers bank accounts. A real man of the people! Then in true woke hypocritical fashion he condemns authoritarian governments around the world, you could not make it up! he is truly the epitome of the clown world compromised tyrannical politician, who shields himself with woke political correctness nonsense (25).

What can we do? As stated before the best way is mass noncompliance, don't try and push all this information on your slave minded colleagues or family members, they'll not listen, instead drop hints and ask them questions, make them think for themselves, make them think critically, I can tell you they're not used to it! We need to reject their media platforms, we need to stop using their money, that way they can't control us. We need to stop paying the governments tax to use against us. They are nothing without us! We already have all the tools to reject the new world order, we just need everyone to wake up and start using the tools that will secure our continued freedom as a population and generation. You'll get people saying you're mad, they wouldn't do this, but the answer is you wouldn't do this but they would and have on multiple occasions. I believe all these agendas are connected, if you delve deep they are all funded by the same few elite billionaires. The woke agenda is for the purpose of censorship and ridicule of anyone questioning the narrative, the vaccines are to enable the vaccine passport and social credit system, the gender ideology is to break up the family unit, the feminist agenda is to stop women staying at home to bring up their children, they now think a career is more rewarding than to bring up a family, leaving the children in public schools to be indoctrinated with radical ideology. It's all geared towards the elitist great reset and obeying the elitist authority and anti-humanist agenda. One man taking a lead role in every tyrannical agenda is

Bill Gates. Bill, once a disgraced computer mogul, who went down in court facing charges of copyright came back out of obscurity to be the world's most generous man, the world's greatest medical mind, doctor and philanthropist, he also gets more air time than an albatross, almost like he owns all the media companies, oh wait!. This is the tried and tested tool of rebranding yourself as a saint, the same tactic used by the infamous John D Rockefeller. Its strange how Bill seems to have his hands in everything nefarious, he seems to be the leading expert and investor in vaccines, he's buying up all the farm land, writing books on climate change, he's so talented to be an expert on all this central planning, almost like he was a charlatan not a philanthropist. Bill Gates father was a Rockefeller employee and billionaire; he was also the head of Planned Parenthood in the US, which was rebranded from The Eugenics League when the name became a little risky as history progressed. Bill is not a computer genius, he's backed by wealthy daddy and only bought the code for Microsoft for $50,000, and he's purely a chancer. Maybe he's still inspired by his father's work in eugenics? (V25a). The same could be said for Mark Zuckerberg, he didn't invent Facebook at University as the story suggests, Facebook is run by the CIA, think about it, a site where everyone writes their lives every detail, it's a CIA dream. Not only that but they sell your data for copious amounts of money to advertising companies and the likes, I deleted mine a few years ago and I'd it's the best thing I ever did! No more low IQ squabbles and moaning, why do you want to see that? I've moved onto Twitter which you'll still find the odd low IQ troll but the debate and conversation is a far higher level of IQ. Since Elon Musk has taken over it's also a much more pleasurable experience with more free speech and debate, hard science from scientists and independent journalist with great content.

If you don't think these elites are capable of these atrocities look no further than what happened on the day of 9/11 2001, an official story with more holes than a net, I'm not sure what happened that day but looking at the evidence I'm pretty certain it was a false flag attack on their own people to enable public support to invade Afghanistan. 7 Buildings went down that day from 2 planes not two, which is the public consensus, this 5 minute video from the brilliant James Corbett of the Corbett Report (highly recommended) outlines the sheer hypocrisy of the official 9/11 story, if anyone still believes it after watching the video I'd suggest they were a few prawns short of a cocktail! (V26).

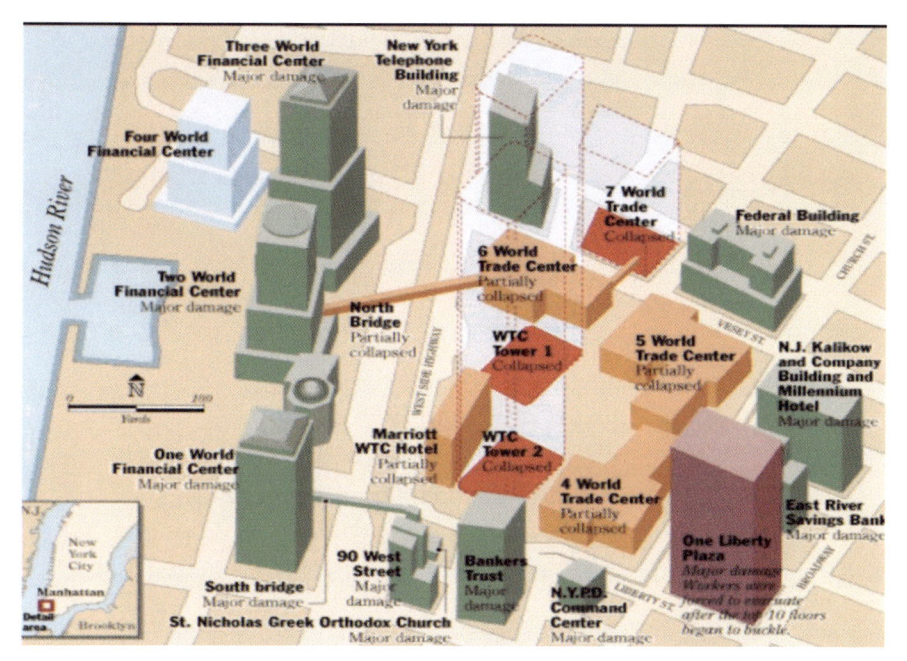

I better end here in fear of being labelled a conspiracy theorist, although I prefer the terms conspiracy realist or conspiracy researcher. I hope you will now question the narrative of the day and realise the importance of freedom, never be tricked into trading your freedom for safety! Freedom is and always has been humanities greatest asset, it's not been that way for the majority of history and we can't let tyrants take our most privileged asset we have away from us. There is a war between decentralisation and centralised authority, elites don't want to let go of their centralised power, things will get rocky before they get better. Our past generations and ancestors fought and gave their life for our freedom and we are only hanging onto it, in the US via the constitution and by human rights laws in the UK courts, if they were to go it would be full scale tyranny, it takes considerable knowledge to realise the extent of your own ignorance, stay vigilant!!!

# References

- 1. UK Influenza Pandemic Preparedness Strategy - https://assets.publishing.service.gov.uk/government/uploads/system/uploads/attachment_data/file/213717/dh_131040.pdf

- 2. 18 reasons I won't be getting a Covid Vaccine - https://www.sott.net/article/451497-18-reasons-I-wont-be-getting-a-Covid-Vaccine See Also - Immunization with SARS Coronavirus Vaccines Leads to Pulmonary Immunopathology on Challenge with the SARS Virus - https://pdfs.semanticscholar.org/962c/58e6dc9c1ea550eb51ce70b0d7c83dc7eff6.pdf

- 3. Infection fatality rate of COVID-19 in community-dwelling populations with emphasis on the elderly: An overview - https://www.medrxiv.org/content/10.1101/2021.07.08.21260210v1

- 4. Continued Effectiveness of COVID-19 Vaccination among Urban Healthcare Workers during Delta Variant Predominance - https://www.medrxiv.org/content/10.1101/2021.11.15.21265753v1

- 5. The Great Barrington Declaration - https://gbdeclaration.org/

- 6. Timeline of government interventions and events regarding the COVID-19 pandemic in Sweden January 31, 2019, to June 3, 2021. - https://zenodo.org/record/5718433#.YsMFPhbhvDs

- 7. National Vaccine Information Centre - https://www.medalerts.org/vaersdb/findfield.php?TABLE=ON
- 8. Electronic Support for Public Health–Vaccine Adverse Event Reporting System (ESP:VAERS) - https://icandecide.org/wp-content/uploads/2020/12/Lazarus-report.pdf
- 9. Pfizer to Pay $2.3 Billion for Fraudulent Marketing - https://www.justice.gov/opa/pr/justice-department-announces-largest-health-care-fraud-settlement-its-history
- 10 Johnson & Johnson to Pay More Than $2.2 Billion to Resolve Criminal and Civil Investigations - https://www.justice.gov/opa/pr/johnson-johnson-pay-more-22-billion-resolve-criminal-and-civil-investigations
- 11. Pharmaceutical Giant AstraZeneca to Pay $520 Million for Off-label Drug Marketing - https://www.justice.gov/opa/pr/pharmaceutical-giant-astrazeneca-pay-520-million-label-drug-marketing
- 12. COVID-19 Vaccine AstraZeneca Vaccine Analysis Print - https://assets.publishing.service.gov.uk/government/uploads/system/uploads/attachment_data/file/1121352/COVID-19_Vaccine_AstraZeneca_VAP.pdf
- 13. 5.3.6 CUMULATIVE ANALYSIS OF POST-AUTHORIZATION ADVERSE EVENT REPORTS OF PF-07302048 (BNT162B2) RECEIVED THROUGH 28-FEB-2021 - https://phmpt.org/wp-content/uploads/2021/11/5.3.6-postmarketing-experience.pdf
- 14. Bill & Melinda Gates Committed Grants - https://www.gatesfoundation.org/about/committed-grants?page=5
- 15. Dissolving Illusions Disease, Vaccines, and the Forgotten History - https://dissolvingillusions.com/wp-content/uploads/2021/07/Dissolving-Illusions-Disease-Vaccines-and-The-Forgotten-History-FREE-Chapters-.pdf

- 16. US Vaccine Excipient Summary - https://www.cdc.gov/vaccines/pubs/pinkbook/downloads/appendices/B/excipient-table-2.pdf

- 17. Cumulative inactivated vaccine exposure and allergy development among children: a birth cohort from Japan - https://www.ncbi.nlm.nih.gov/pmc/articles/PMC7341599/

- 18. Relative Incidence of Office Visits and Cumulative Rates of Billed Diagnoses Along the Axis of Vaccination - https://www.ncbi.nlm.nih.gov/pmc/articles/PMC7709050/

- 19. Let's Compare the Vaccinated to the Unvaccinated - https://yummy.doctor/video-list/lets-compare-the-vaccinated-to-the-unvaccinated/

- 20. What you Didn't Know about Polio - https://rodneydodson000.medium.com/what-you-didnt-know-about-polio-26d20cba98e5

- 21. The Smallpox Pandemic was Eerily Similar to Covid - https://amidwesterndoctor.substack.com/p/the-smallpox-pandemic-response-was?utm_source=url HYPERLINK "https://amidwesterndoctor.substack.com/p/the-smallpox-

- 22. H.R.5546 - National Childhood Vaccine Injury Act of 1986 - https://www.congress.gov/bill/99th-congress/house-bill/5546

- 23. Annual summary of vital statistics of the 20th century - https://www.researchgate.net/publication/12227539_Annual_Summary_of_Vital_Statistics_Trends_in_the_Health_of_Americans_During_the_20th_Century

- 24. Correlation Between 3790 Quantitative Polymerase Chain Reaction–Positives Samples and Positive Cell Cultures, Including 1941 Severe Acute Respiratory Syndrome Coronavirus 2 Isolates - https://academic.oup.com/cid/article/72/11/e921/5912603

- 25. Coronavirus: Devon schools closed as Cornwall has first COVID-19 case - https://www.devonlive.com/news/devon-news/live-coronavirus-devon-cornwall-latest-3920681

- 26. No Significant Difference in Viral Load Between Vaccinated and Unvaccinated, Asymptomatic and Symptomatic Groups Infected with SARS-CoV-2 Delta Variant - https://www.medrxiv.org/content/10.1101/2021.09.28.21264262v1

- 27. COVID-19: stigmatising the unvaccinated is not justified - https://www.thelancet.com/journals/lancet/article/PIIS0140-6736(21)02243-1/fulltext

- 28. Transmission of 2019-nCoV Infection from an Asymptomatic Contact in Germany - https://www.nejm.org/doi/full/10.1056/NEJMc2001468

- 29. Are Face Masks Effective? The Evidence. - https://swprs.org/face-masks-evidence/

- 30. Thread: THE TWITTER FILES - https://twitter.com/mtaibbi/status/1598822959866683394?s=46

- 30a Cherry Picked Climate & Temperature Data
  https://realclimatescience.com/61-fake-data/

- 31 Climate Scientists - No Crisis
  https://clintel.org/wp-content/uploads/2022/06/WCD-version-06272215121.pdf

- 32 Climate Crisis Consensus
  https://co2coalition.org/2021/10/31/97-consensus-what-consensus/

- 33 BP Carbon Footprint Greenwashing
  https://greenisthenewblack.com/carbon-footprint-bp/

- 34 Climategate Emails
  https://noconsensus.wordpress.com/2011/11/22/climategate-2-0/

- 35 IPCC Climate Data Report

https://www.ipcc.ch/site/assets/uploads/2018/03/ipcc_far_wg_I_chapter_07-1.pdf

- 36 Nasa Ozone Layer Data
  https://ozonewatch.gsfc.nasa.gov/statistics/ytd_data.txt

- 37 What is Medicines 5 sigma?
  https://www.thelancet.com/journals/lancet/article/PIIS0140-6736(15)60696-1/fulltext

# Interactive Video References

V1. Chinese Dropping Dead in Street Due to Covid - https://twitter.com/basedasfcuk/status/1500370284557307905?s=46

V2. Dr. Peter McCullough with Joe Rogan – The Joe Rogan Experience #1747 - https://odysee.com/@FUNWO:5/Dr-Peter-McCullough-with-Joe-Rogan-%E2%80%93-The-Joe-Rogan-Experience--1747:3

V3. Bill Gates 2010 TED talk - Lowering Population with New Vaccines - https://odysee.com/@grok-sword:9/bill.gates.ted.2010.lower.population.new.vaccines:7

V4. Vaccines Stop COVID Transmission The Clown World Show - https://odysee.com/@alltheworldsastage:0/Vaccines-Stop-COVID-Transmission-The-Clown-World-Show:3

V5. The Speed of Science Feat. Janine Small (Pfizer) - https://odysee.com/@ursachenforschung-gtz:9/Der-niederl%C3%A4ndische-Abgeordnete-Rob-Roos-wollte-von-der-Pfizer-Direktorin-Janine-Small-wissen,:f

V6. On Midazolam, 'End of Life "Care" Pathways' & the Nursing Code of Conduct - https://odysee.com/@MaajidNawaz:d/EP27-Radical:8

V7. DR. Karry Mullis on PCR testing - https://odysee.com/@odysseus:b8/Karry-Mullis-PCR:b

V8. Dr. Karry Mullis on Anthony Fauci - https://odysee.com/@ProgressiveTruthSeekers:3/Dr-Kary-Mullis-on-Anthony-Fauci:3

V9. Australia Has Fallen - For Their Health & Safety - https://odysee.com/@deehinja:5/Oxbasfallen:3

V10. 60 Minutes: Dr. Facui on wearing masks - https://odysee.com/@Activist.net.nz:2/60-Minutes-Dr-Fauci-on-wearing-masks:d

V11. BBC Newsnight Deb Cohen - Masks Unscientific and Political WHO Lobbying - https://odysee.com/@deehinja:5/Debcohen:b

V12. TIKTOK Nurses Dancing Mayhem War Zones Hospitals Covid-19 Pandemic - https://odysee.com/@alltheworldsastage:0/PanAdmin-PART2-Dancing-Nurses-Covid-19-Coronavirus-Lockdowns-Masks-Quarantine-Pandemic-Curfews:2

V13. The Empty Hospitals of 2020 Compilation - https://odysee.com/@CosmicEvent:5/EMPTY-HOSPITALS-A-SHORT-TRIP-DOWN-MEMORY-LANE:3

V14. Pots And Pans Thursday - V15. The vaccinated trying to shame the unvaccinated: - https://twitter.com/tythefisch/status/1438666481626144769?s=46

V16. 2000 Mules (2022) - https://odysee.com/@BannedYouTubeVideos:4/2000-Mules-2022:a

V17. Joe Biden - Gaffe after Gaffe after Gaffe - https://odysee.com/@MAGAlionHAT:e/Joe-Biden---Gaffe-after-Gaffe---MLH:4

V17a. Joe Biden Gaffs https://odysee.com/@MAGAlionHAT:e/Joe-Biden---Gaffe-after-Gaffe---MLH:4

V17b. Presidents Kennedy's Final Speech https://twitter.com/wikileaksus/status/1588756579662585856?s=46&t=l2bS2U44JWmyyMB9oVc7PA

V18. Pro-Choice Hypocrisy Will Shock You -
https://twitter.com/OzraeliAvi/status/1548615485805441024?s=20

V19. Greenland Ice Core Data -
https://twitter.com/deehinja/status/1560920114303737856?s=46

V20. Governments and Elites Stating Vaccines Stop Transmission
https://twitter.com/deehinja/status/1559654095429959686?s=46&t=l2bS2U44JWmyyMB9oVc7PA

V21. US Politicians an Media View on Covid Vaccine When Trump was President
https://twitter.com/deehinja/status/1559654387190054914?s=46&t=l2bS2U44JWmyyMB9oVc7PA

V22. BBC Running The World News Alliance
https://twitter.com/deehinja/status/1557377511771734016?s=46&t=l2bS2U44JWmyyMB9oVc7PA

V23. Thomas Sowell & Milton Friedman on Inflation
Thomas Sowell -
https://twitter.com/deehinja/status/1560161706457894912?s=46&t=l2bS2U44JWmyyMB9oVc7PA

Milton Freidman -
https://twitter.com/deehinja/status/1575937797466206209?s=46&t=l2bS2U44JWmyyMB9oVc7PA

V24. Bill Gates a Major Doner to Fact Checking Organisations - Corbett Report
https://twitter.com/deehinja/status/1559935738011058177?s=46&t=l2bS2U44JWmyyMB9oVc7PA

V24a. Julian Assange on Endless Wars
https://twitter.com/wikileaks/status/1645774558295728130?s=20

V25. Trudeu Hypocrisy
https://twitter.com/jamesmelville/status/1627951617210298369?s=46&t=l2bS2U44JWmyyMB9oVc7PA

[V25a Who is Bill Gates – The Corbett Report](https://odysee.com/@JohnDeaux:8/2020-who-is-bill-gates:b)

[V26. James Corbett - 9/11 official story in 5 Minutes](https://odysee.com/@TabooConspiracy:c/5-minute-9-11-commemoration:2)

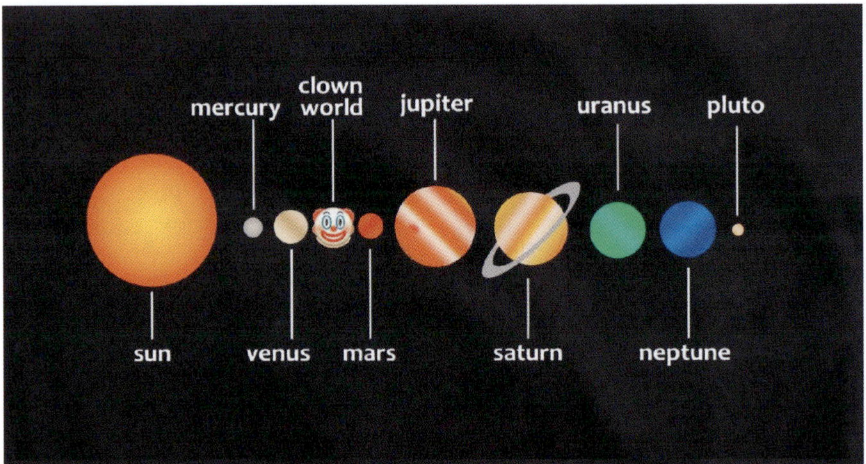
mercury
clown world
jupiter
uranus
pluto
sun
venus
mars
saturn
neptune

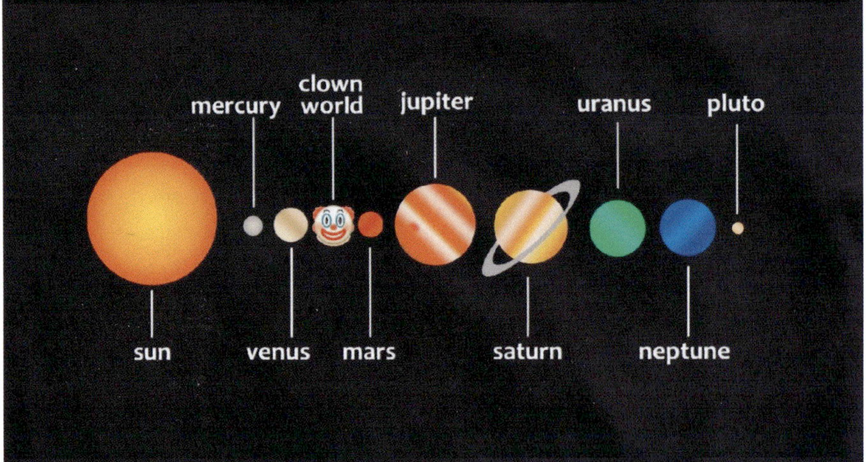
mercury
clown world
jupiter
uranus
pluto
sun
venus
mars
saturn
neptune

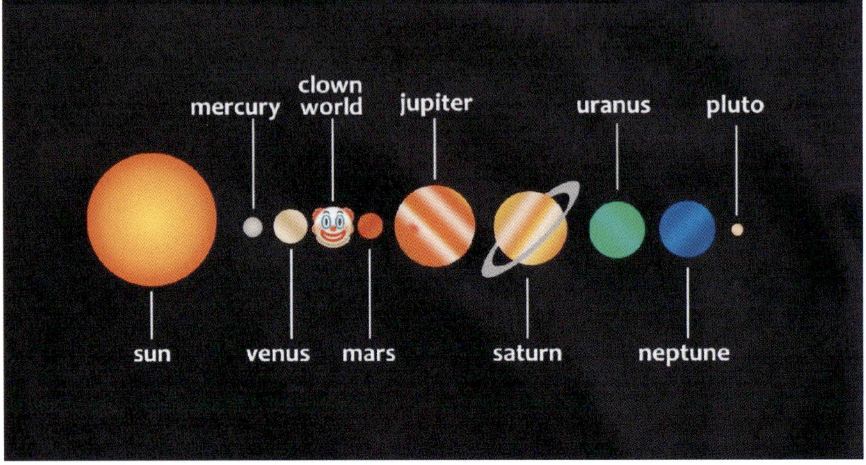
mercury
clown world
jupiter
uranus
pluto
sun
venus
mars
saturn
neptune

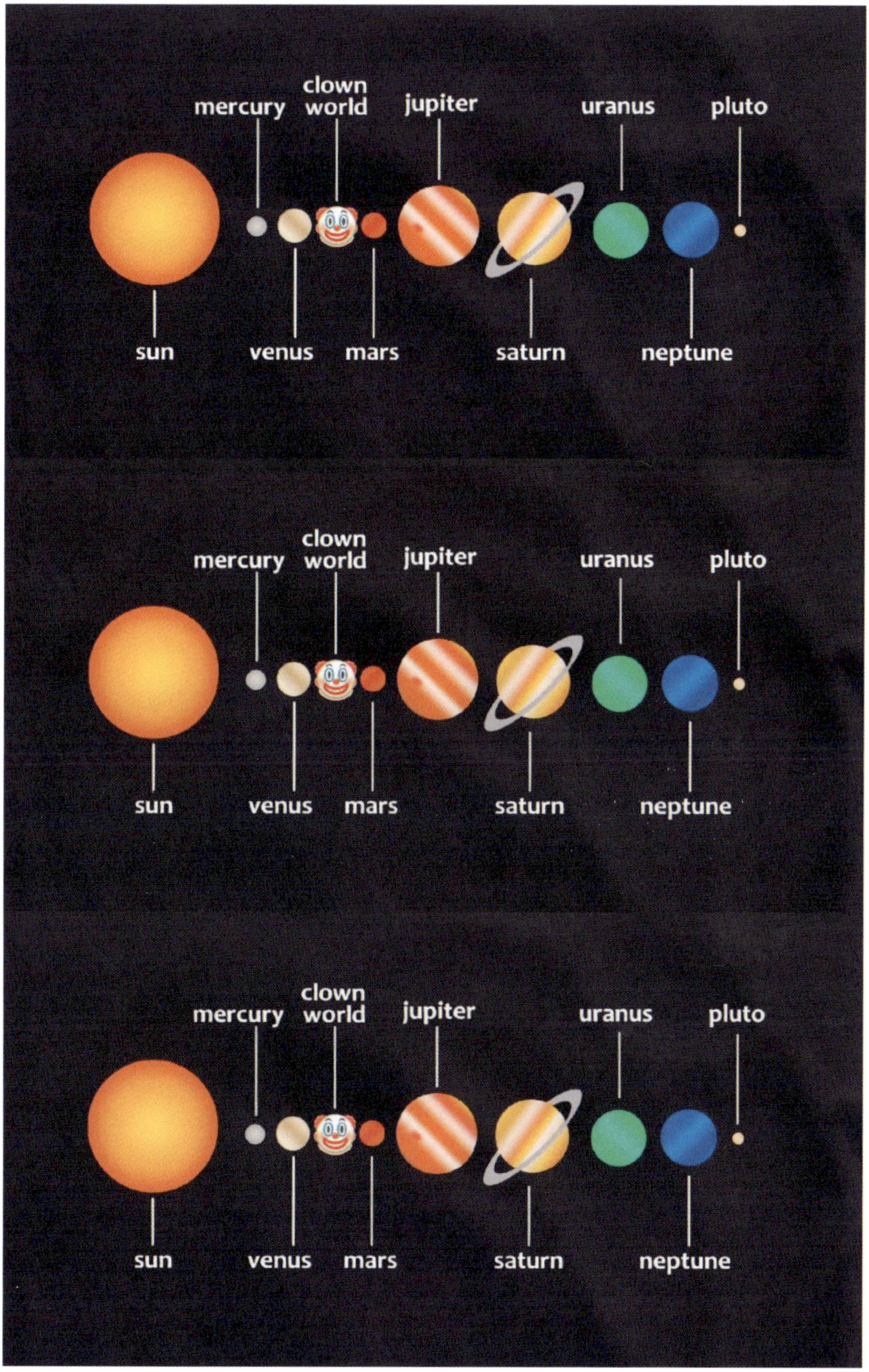
clown world
mercury
jupiter
uranus
pluto
sun
venus
mars
saturn
neptune
clown world
mercury
jupiter
uranus
pluto
sun
venus
mars
saturn
neptune
clown world
mercury
jupiter
uranus
pluto
sun
venus
mars
saturn
neptune

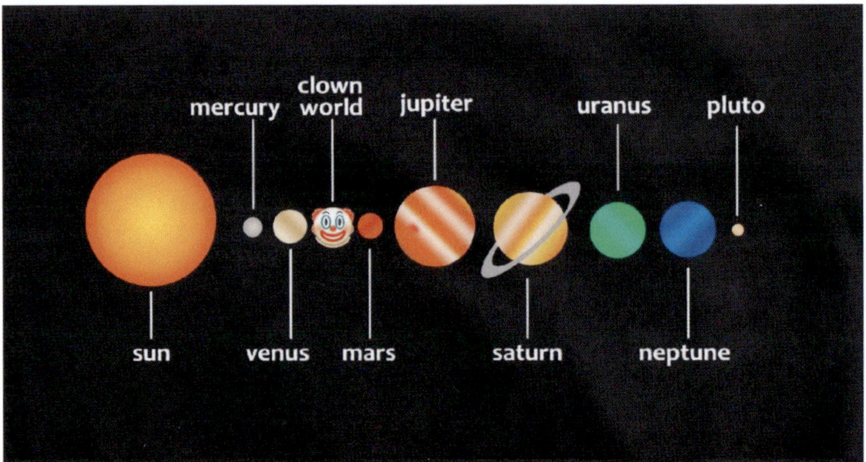
clown world
mercury
jupiter
uranus
pluto
sun
venus
mars
saturn
neptune

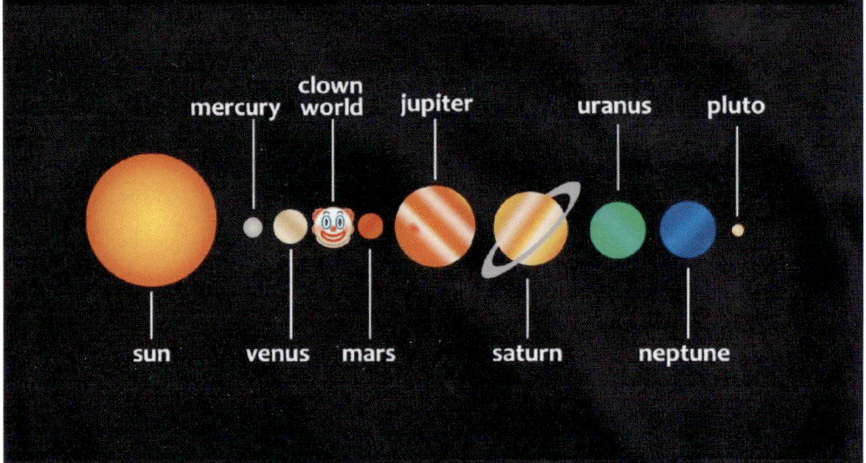
clown world
mercury
jupiter
uranus
pluto
sun
venus
mars
saturn
neptune

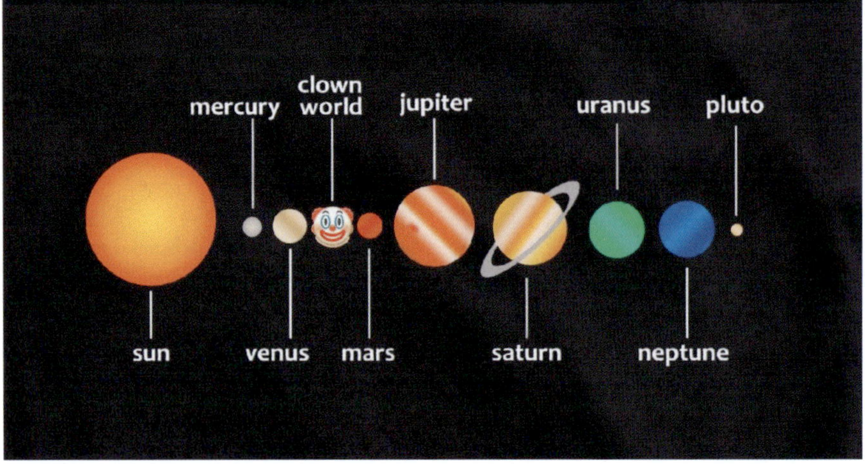
clown world
mercury
jupiter
uranus
pluto
sun
venus
mars
saturn
neptune

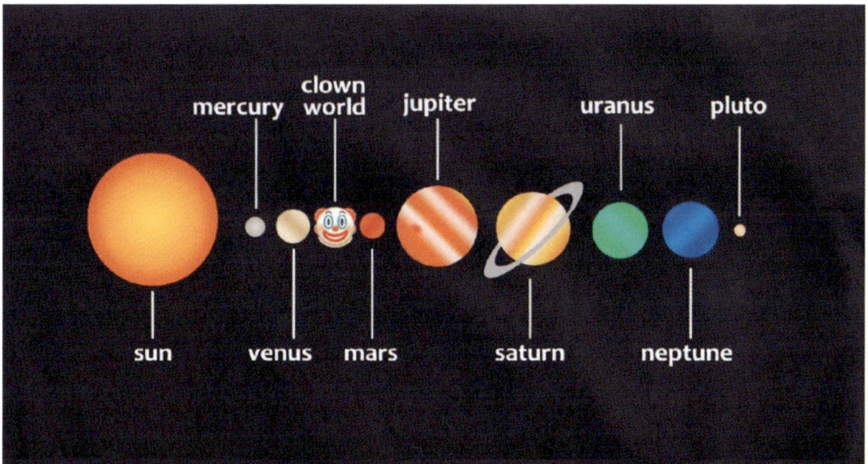
mercury
clown world
jupiter
uranus
pluto
sun
venus
mars
saturn
neptune

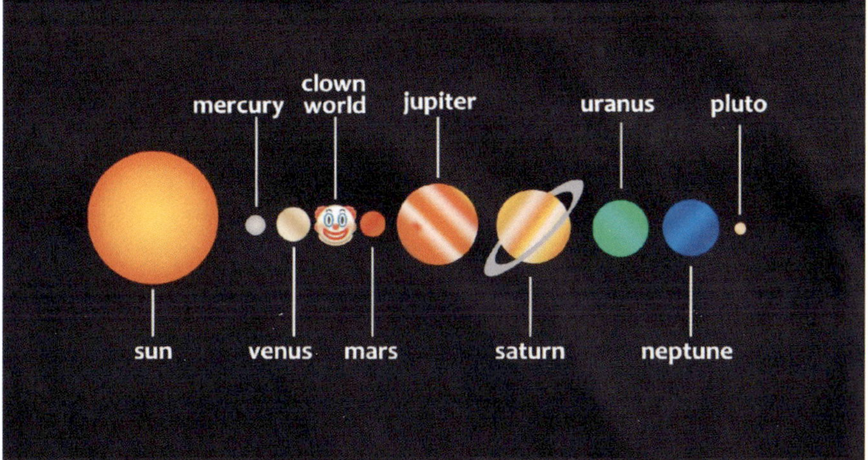
mercury
clown world
jupiter
uranus
pluto
sun
venus
mars
saturn
neptune

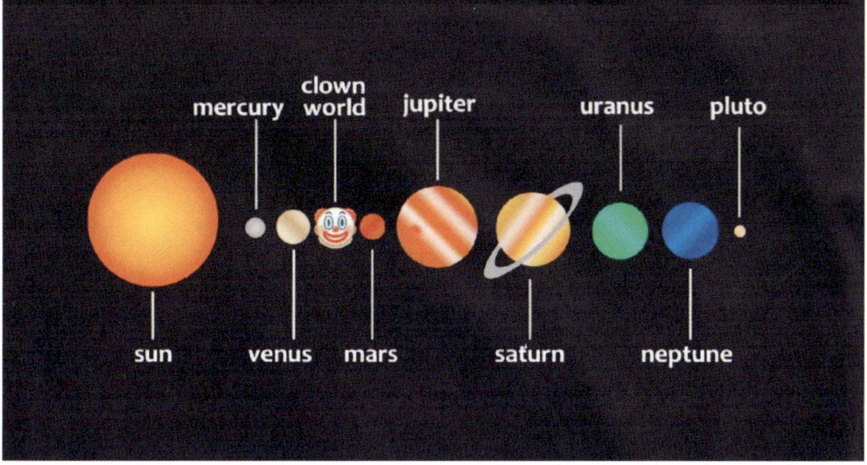
mercury
clown world
jupiter
uranus
pluto
sun
venus
mars
saturn
neptune

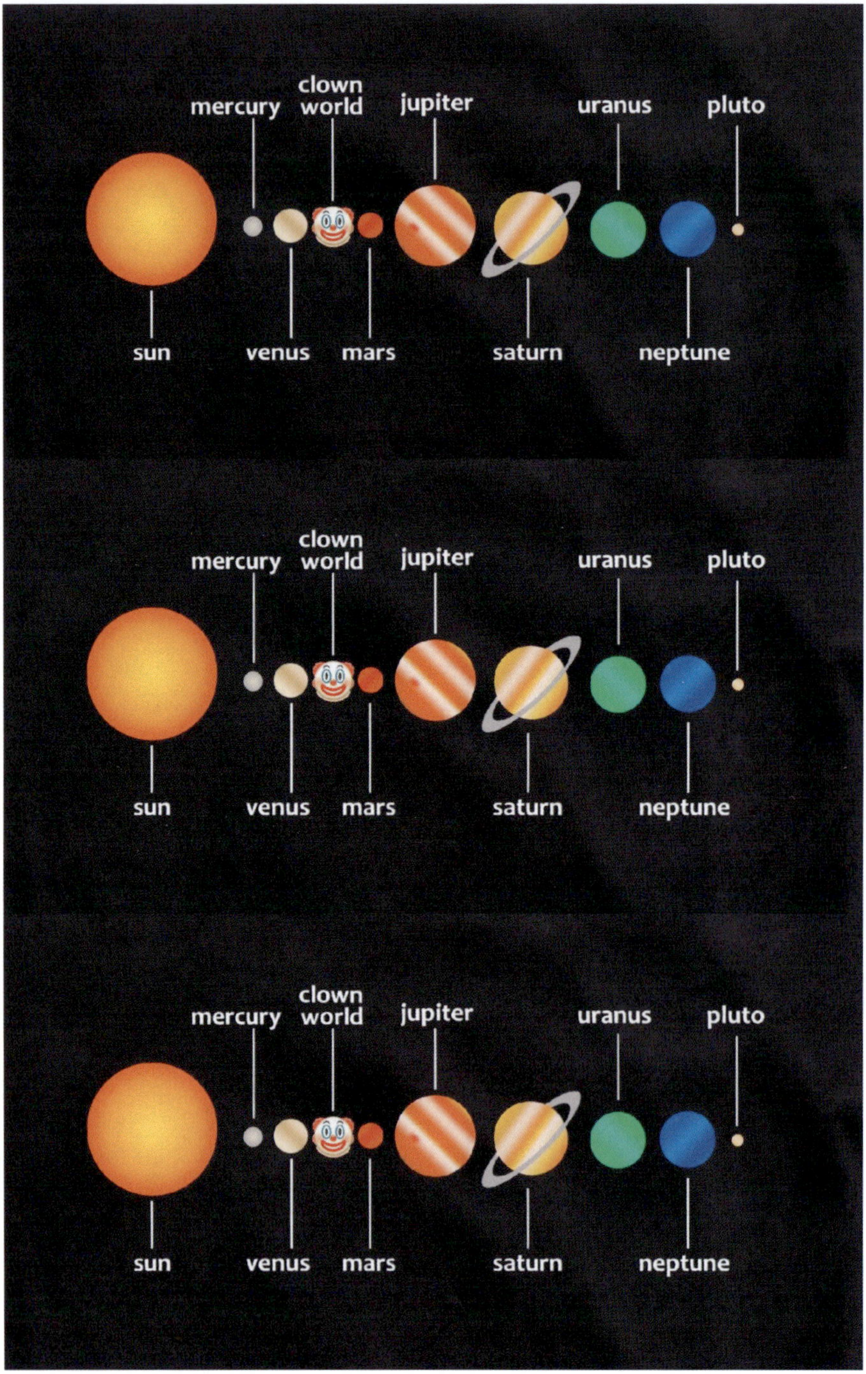
clown world
mercury
jupiter
uranus
pluto
sun
venus
mars
saturn
neptune
clown world
mercury
jupiter
uranus
pluto
sun
venus
mars
saturn
neptune
clown world
mercury
jupiter
uranus
pluto
sun
venus
mars
saturn
neptune

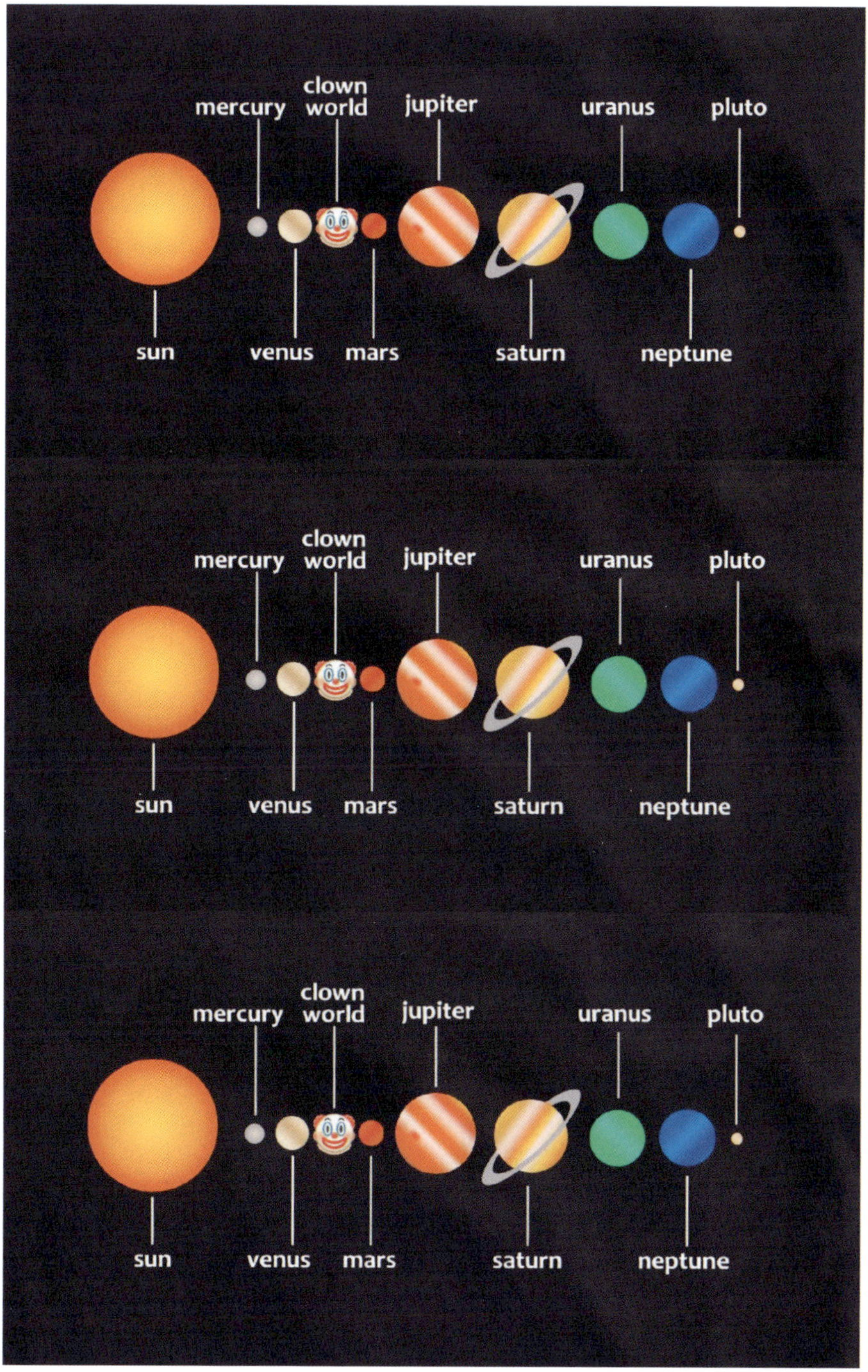
mercury
clown world
jupiter
uranus
pluto
sun
venus
mars
saturn
neptune
mercury
clown world
jupiter
uranus
pluto
sun
venus
mars
saturn
neptune
mercury
clown world
jupiter
uranus
pluto
sun
venus
mars
saturn
neptune

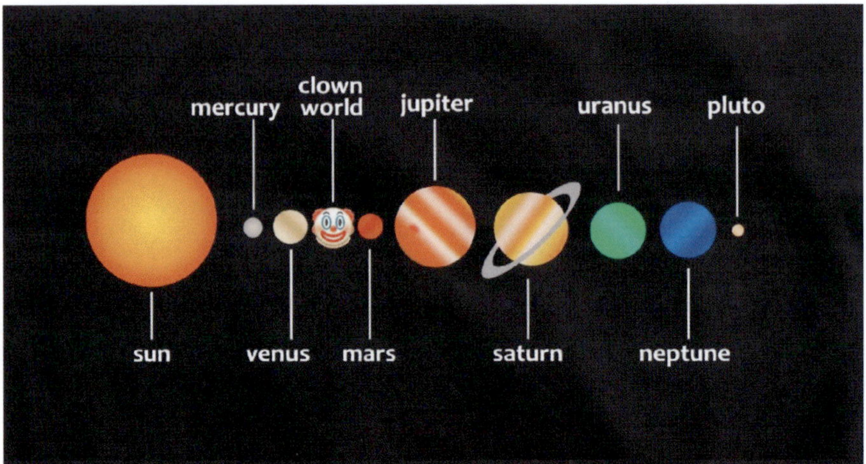
mercury
clown world
jupiter
uranus
pluto
sun
venus
mars
saturn
neptune

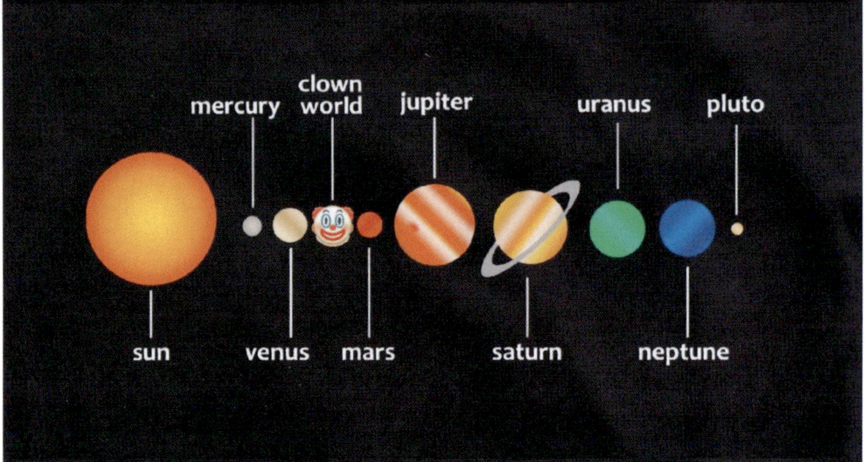
mercury
clown world
jupiter
uranus
pluto
sun
venus
mars
saturn
neptune

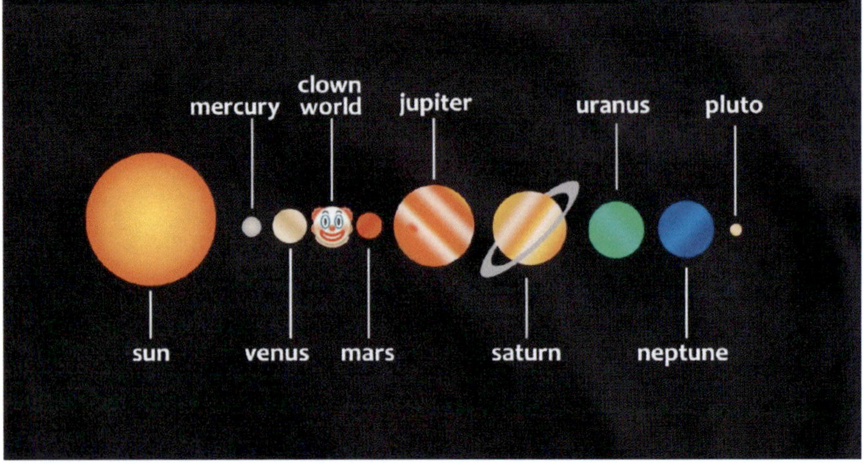
mercury
clown world
jupiter
uranus
pluto
sun
venus
mars
saturn
neptune

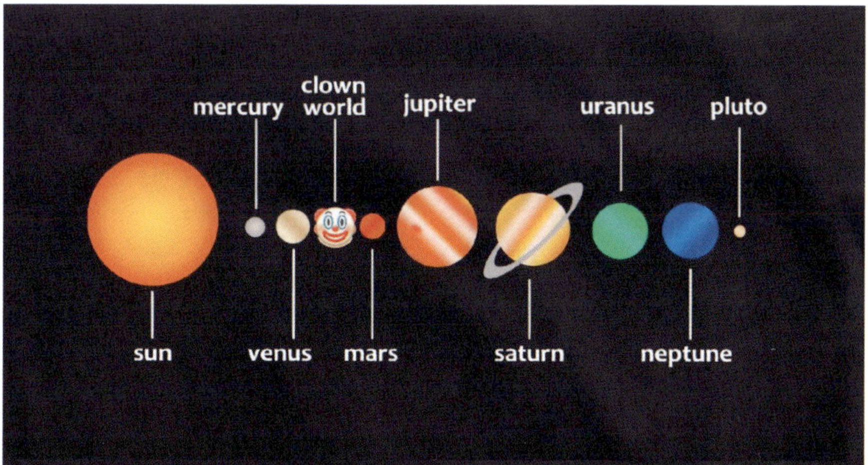
clown world
mercury
jupiter
uranus
pluto
sun
venus
mars
saturn
neptune

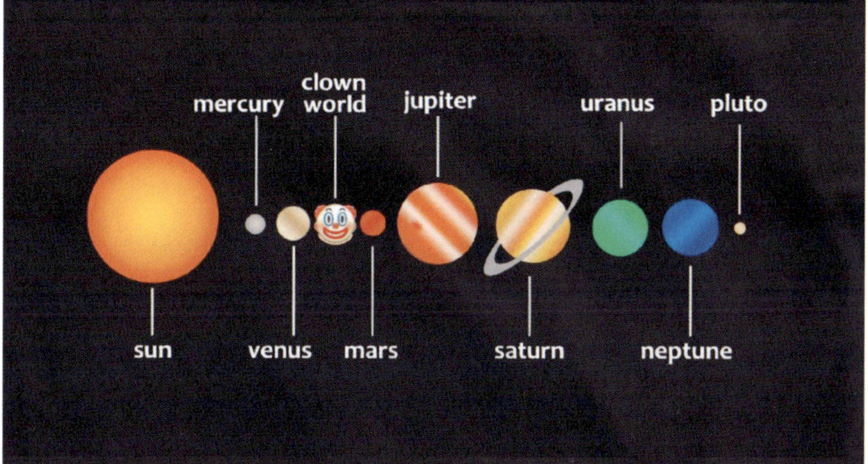
clown world
mercury
jupiter
uranus
pluto
sun
venus
mars
saturn
neptune

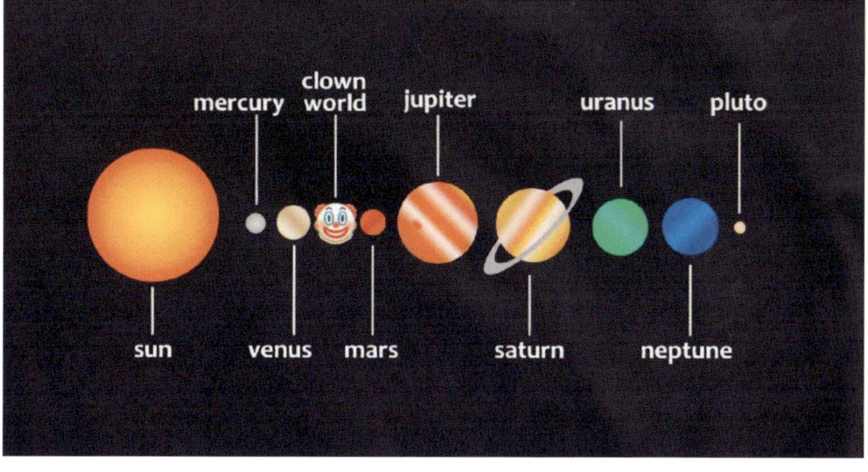
clown world
mercury
jupiter
uranus
pluto
sun
venus
mars
saturn
neptune

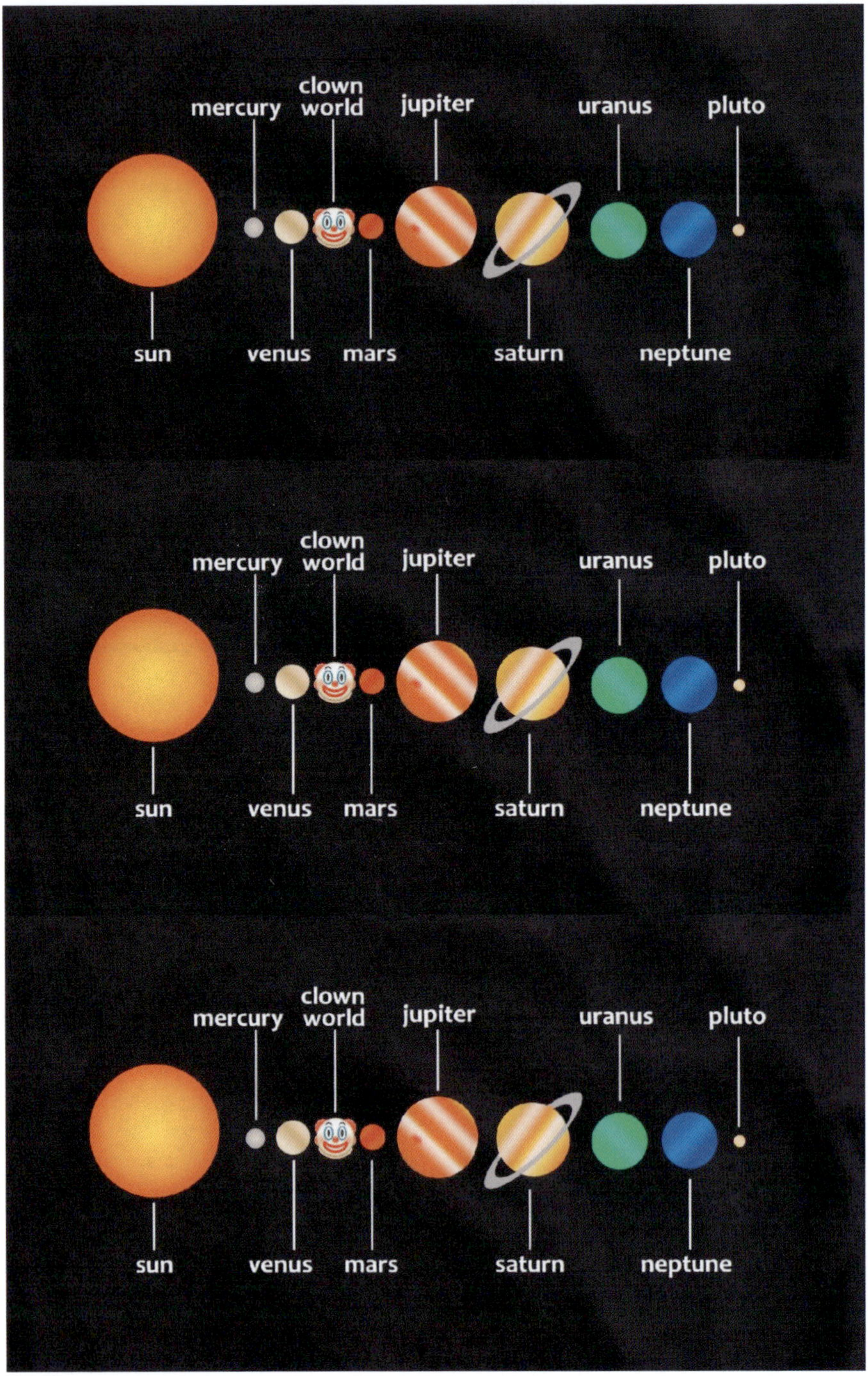
clown world
mercury
jupiter
uranus
pluto
sun
venus
mars
saturn
neptune
clown world
mercury
jupiter
uranus
pluto
sun
venus
mars
saturn
neptune
clown world
mercury
jupiter
uranus
pluto
sun
venus
mars
saturn
neptune

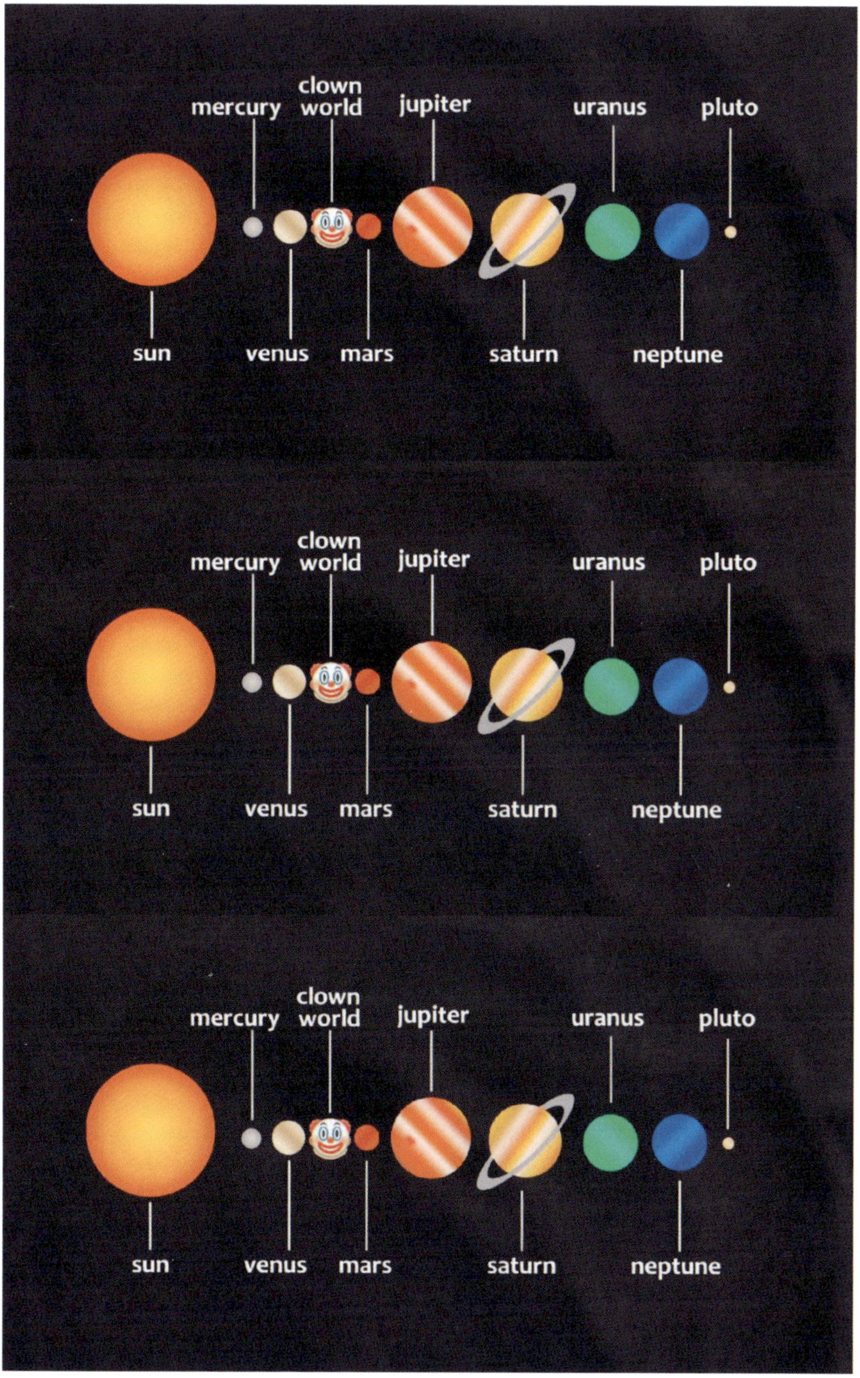
mercury
clown world
jupiter
uranus
pluto
sun
venus
mars
saturn
neptune
mercury
clown world
jupiter
uranus
pluto
sun
venus
mars
saturn
neptune
mercury
clown world
jupiter
uranus
pluto
sun
venus
mars
saturn
neptune

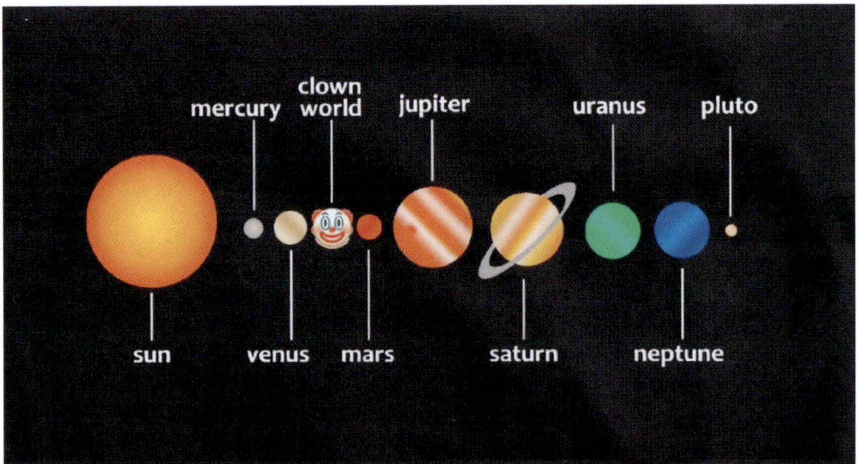
clown world
mercury
jupiter
uranus
pluto
sun
venus
mars
saturn
neptune

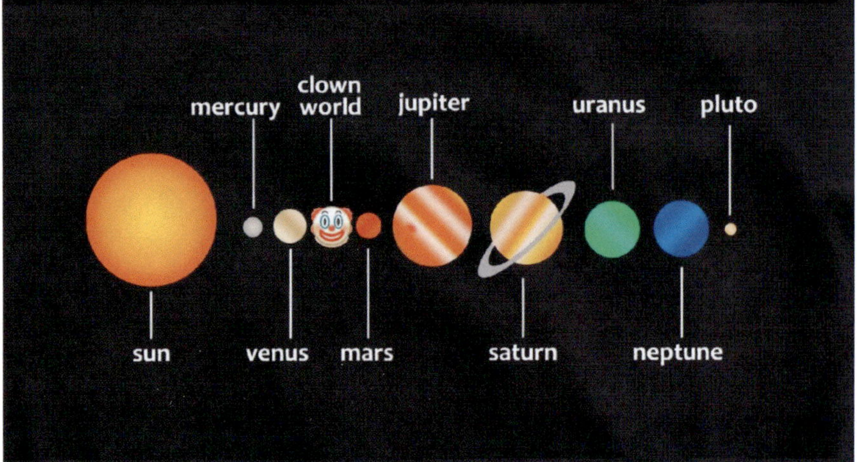
clown world
mercury
jupiter
uranus
pluto
sun
venus
mars
saturn
neptune

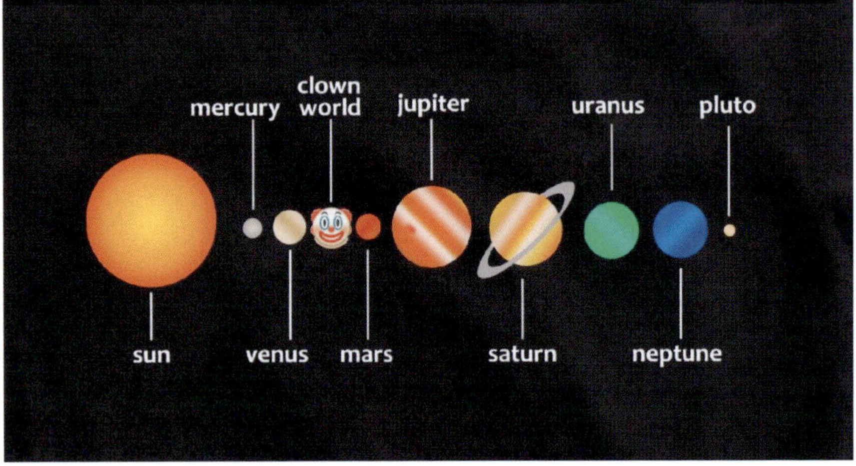
clown world
mercury
jupiter
uranus
pluto
sun
venus
mars
saturn
neptune

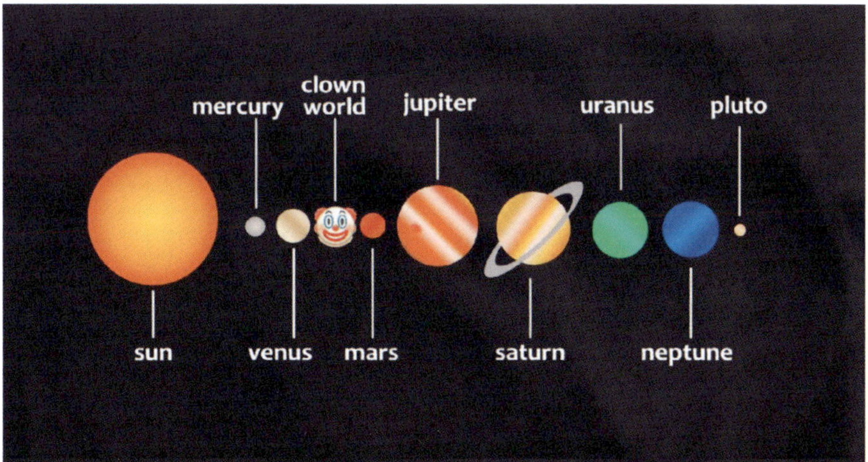
mercury
clown world
jupiter
uranus
pluto
sun
venus
mars
saturn
neptune

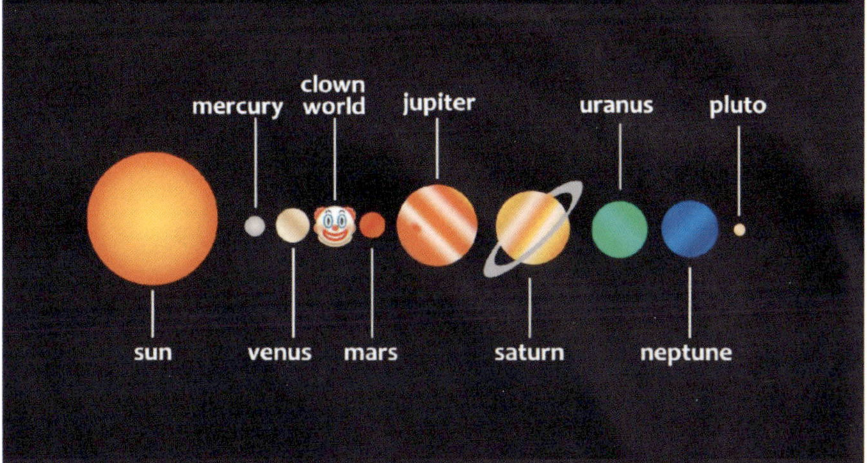
mercury
clown world
jupiter
uranus
pluto
sun
venus
mars
saturn
neptune

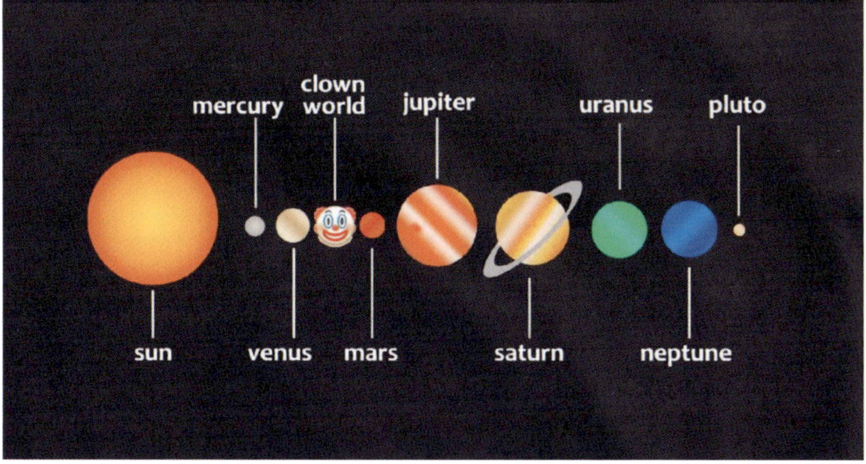
mercury
clown world
jupiter
uranus
pluto
sun
venus
mars
saturn
neptune

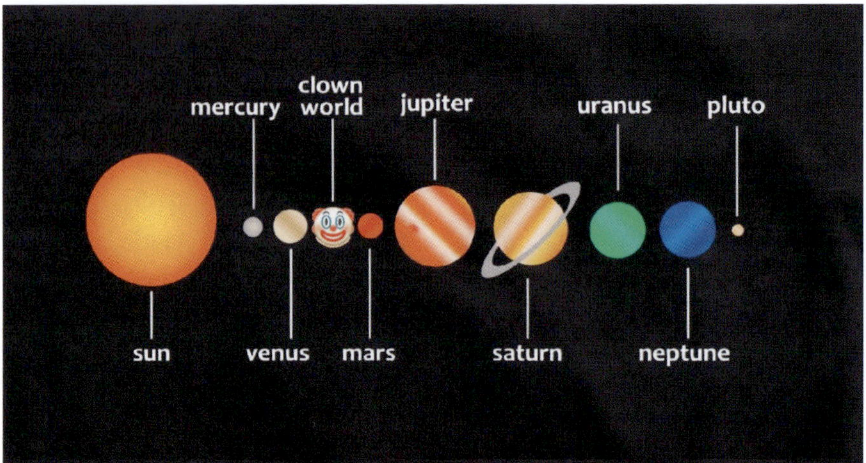
clown world
mercury
jupiter
uranus
pluto
sun
venus
mars
saturn
neptune

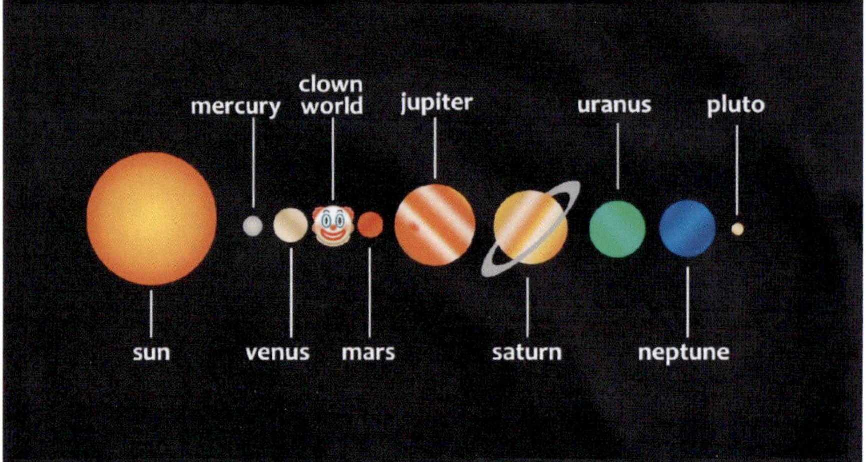
clown world
mercury
jupiter
uranus
pluto
sun
venus
mars
saturn
neptune

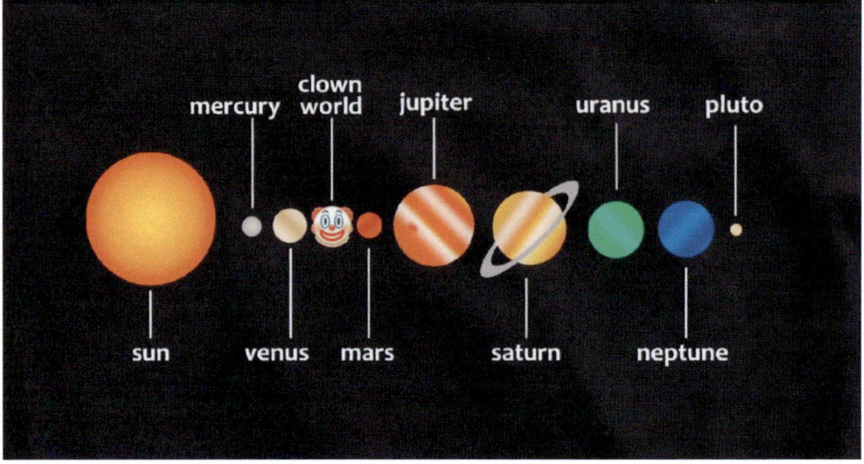
clown world
mercury
jupiter
uranus
pluto
sun
venus
mars
saturn
neptune

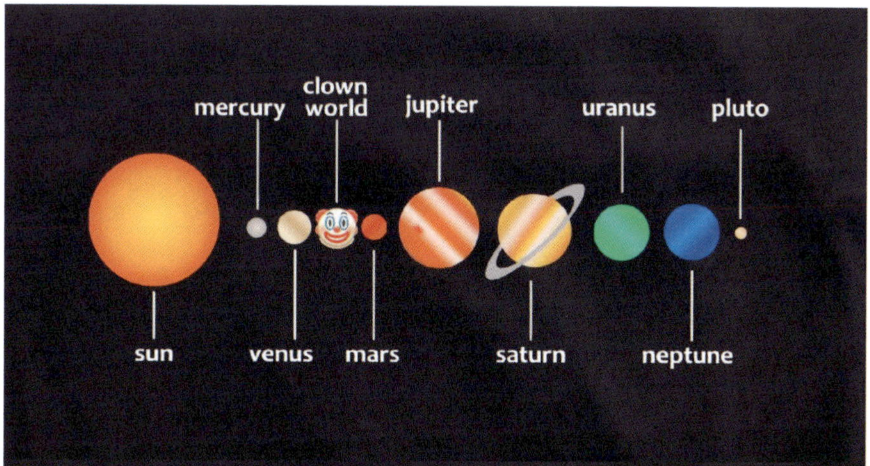
clown world
mercury
jupiter
uranus
pluto
sun
venus
mars
saturn
neptune

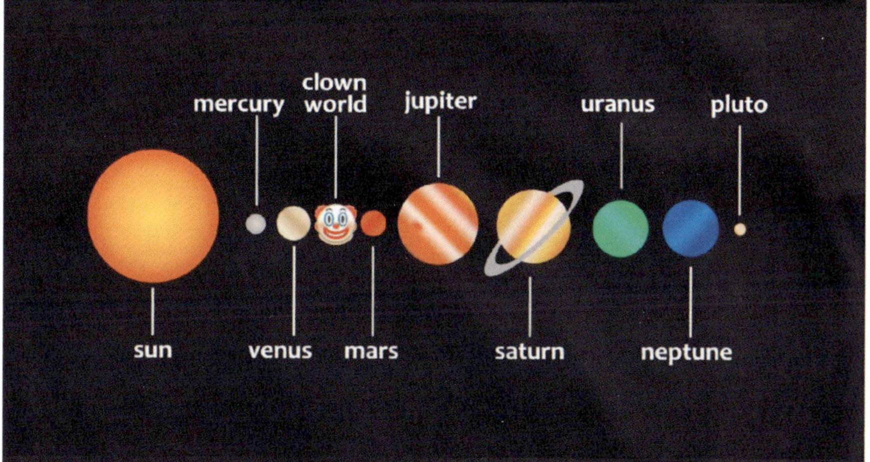
clown world
mercury
jupiter
uranus
pluto
sun
venus
mars
saturn
neptune

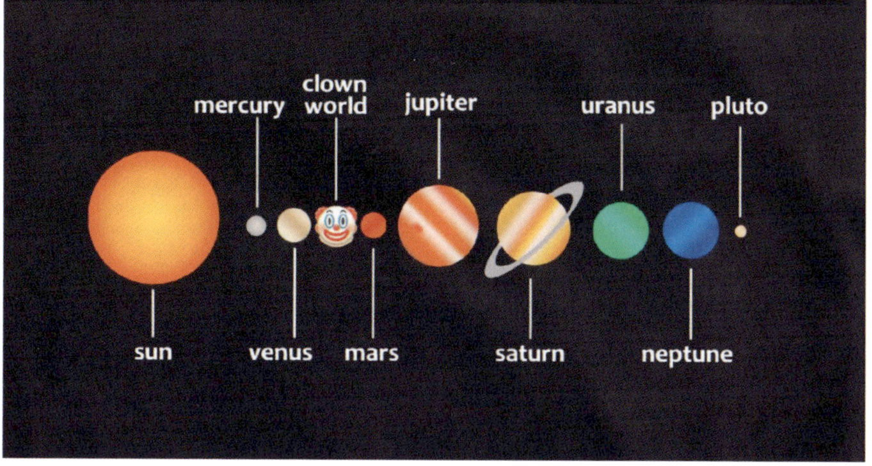
clown world
mercury
jupiter
uranus
pluto
sun
venus
mars
saturn
neptune

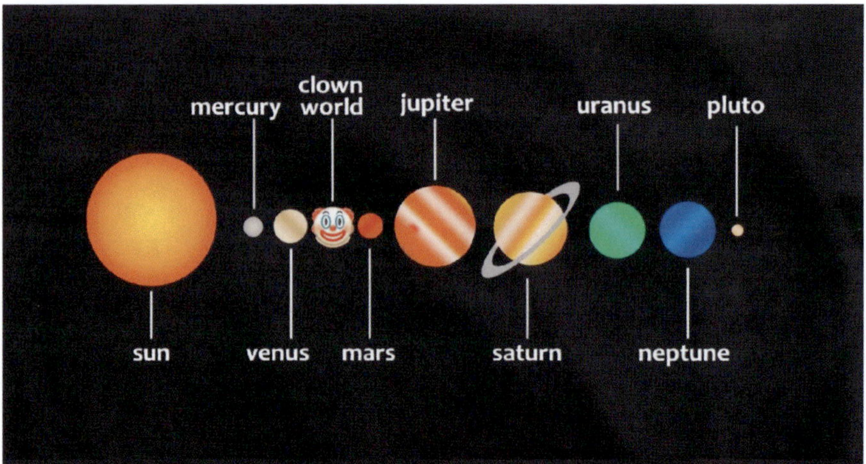
clown
world
mercury
jupiter
uranus
pluto
sun
venus
mars
saturn
neptune

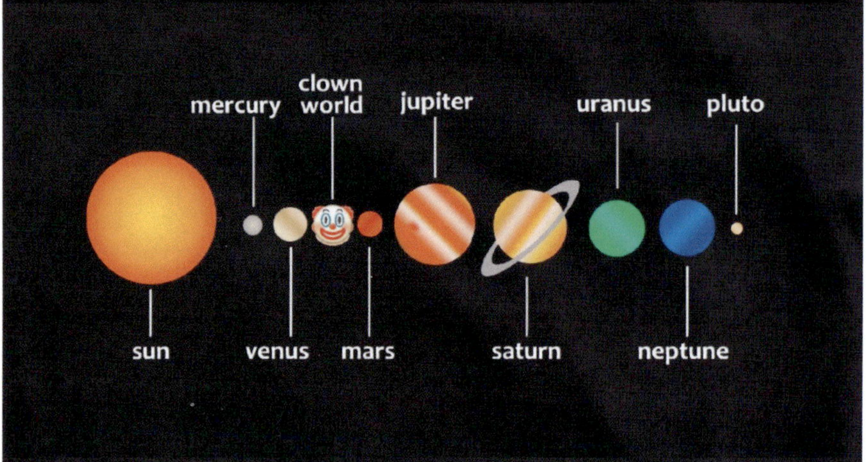
clown
world
mercury
jupiter
uranus
pluto
sun
venus
mars
saturn
neptune

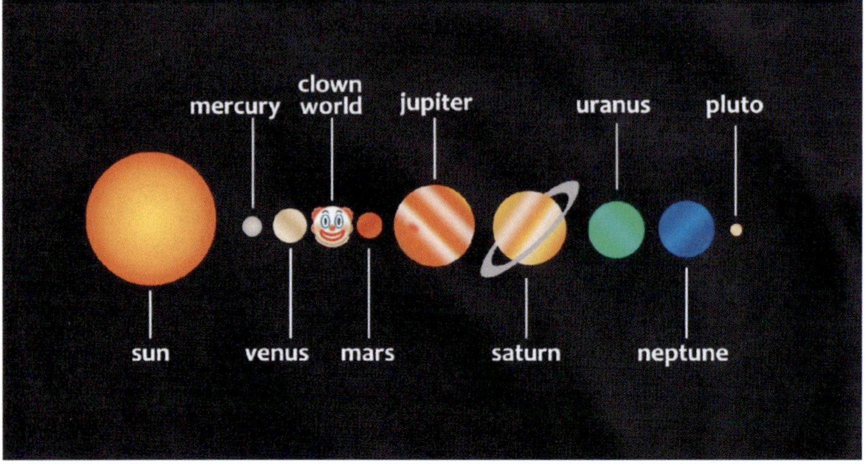
clown
world
mercury
jupiter
uranus
pluto
sun
venus
mars
saturn
neptune

Printed in Poland
by Amazon Fulfillment
Poland Sp. z o.o., Wrocław
22 April 2023

de8f8ebb-69e2-45bb-80ad-9cca6d07fd9cR01